MURDER in
ST. AUGUSTINE

MURDER in ST. AUGUSTINE

THE MYSTERIOUS DEATH OF ATHALIA PONSELL LINDSLEY

ELIZABETH RANDALL

THE
History
PRESS

Published by The History Press
Charleston, SC
www.historypress.net

Copyright © 2016 by Elizabeth Randall
All rights reserved

Cover collage by Bob Randall.

First published 2016

Manufactured in the United States

ISBN 978.1.46711.881.1

Library of Congress Control Number: 2016939312

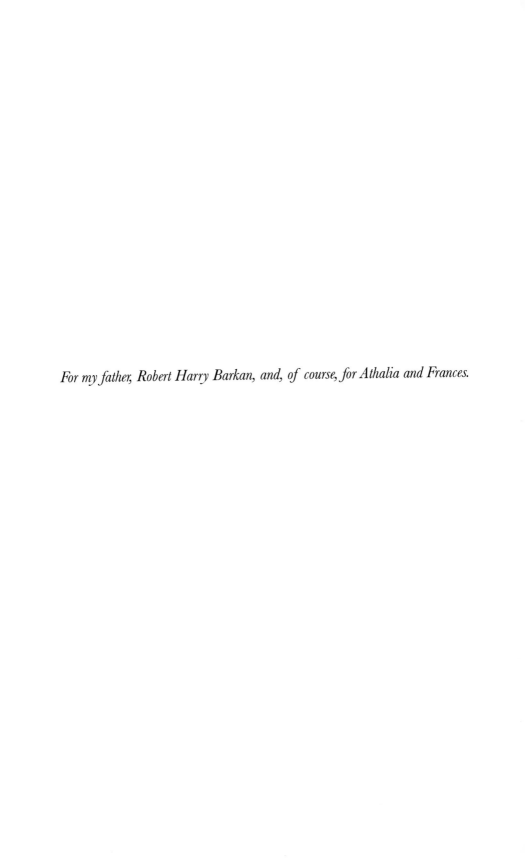

For my father, Robert Harry Barkan, and, of course, for Athalia and Frances.

CONTENTS

From pacifist to terrorist, each person condemns violence—and then adds one cherished case in which it may be justified.

—*Gloria Steinem*

PREFACE

Around 10:00 p.m. on February 24, 1975, in Winter Park, Florida, a shotgun blast shattered the calm of a Monday evening. If the surrounding suburban residents in Winter Park Pines heard anything, they kept it to themselves. The following morning, when a carpet cleaning truck rolled into the driveway of 2911 Montfichet Lane, the result of the ominous noise from the night before was discovered.

The crew of workers came early to pick up invoices from Robert Harry Barkan, a self-employed man who ran his business from the ranch-style house built in the early 1960s. An early riser, Barkan usually greeted the small fleet of trucks and the men spilling out of them, but that morning, the front door remained closed and locked. The carpet cleaning crew heard dogs barking. Something was wrong with the front window, the kitchen window that faced the driveway. The men looked inside. They tried to break down the door. Then they called the police.

The police couldn't get through the front door either, so they went through the window. There they found a gruesome sight: Barkan had been shot in the face through the kitchen window, and he lay dead on his back on the linoleum floor. Beyond him, in the family room, the TV was still on, and a glass of soda, its carbonated bubbles flat, sat beside the recliner.

That moment—a quiet evening at home interrupted, a bloody corpse lying on the floor of a suburban home—became frozen in time; it became, unfortunately, the moment that defined the man. Robert Barkan was a father, a grandfather and a man who served on a navy gunboat during World War

II. He saw the invasion of Leyte in the Philippines at the age of nineteen. Yet to the people who lived after him, Barkan's ignominious death overshadowed every memory of his life, every picture ever taken of him, his beginning, his end and everything in between. Murder has a way of doing that.

Robert Barkan was my father, and when people ask me how he died, I usually say it was an accident. The facts are too complicated to explain. No one was ever charged with his death, and his cold case is still under investigation with the Orange County Sheriff's Department in Orlando, Florida.

I've opened his case from time to time in the ensuing forty years. Once I hired a private detective. The police are pretty sure they know who killed him, but they have no proof. They have no proof because in those days, there were no crime scene units in cities like Winter Park, no DNA testing and no fiber analysis. In the case of my father's murder, police destroyed forensic evidence when they climbed through the kitchen window. The neighbors heard nothing, or so they said. At any rate, no one was talking.

Aside from the shock of losing a parent to such violence, I was stunned by the incongruous nature of the crime. My father lived in a nice house in a nice neighborhood. He was careful to lock up day or night, and he was especially wary at the time of his death because of an attempted robbery in his home two weeks before.

Because of my frustration with the deficiency of evidence and the futility of ever bringing anyone to justice for the crime committed against my father, I became interested in the history of similar homicides. My grandfather Robert Harry Barkan Sr. had been the dean of city police reporters for the *New York Daily Mirror* in the '30s and '40s, and he also freelanced, writing up murder cases for detective magazines. It seemed that I shared a similar aptitude.

I wrote a cover story for an alternative newspaper about local houses where murders had occurred, including 2911 Montfichet Lane. Then I covered the trial of the "X-Box Murders" in Deland for the same newspaper and had several interviews with Troy Victorino, the accused ringleader of the crime. If I couldn't find the criminal who killed my father, I wanted very much to know how a murderer thinks.

What I found out is that a murderer doesn't think differently from anyone else. A murderer is, more likely than not, as sane as you and I. David M. Buss, author of *The Murderer Next Door*, theorizes that murder is an evolutionary adaptation employed most often in matters of pride, greed or lust. What I found out is that murderers and potential murderers swim through society largely unrecognized. Almost everyone has the potential to kill, and labeling this primal urge as "mental illness" misses the point. Perhaps a person who refrains from violence or who seeks alternatives to deadly conflict is the one who is different. I do not believe that people who place little value on human life are unusual or that they can be changed. When they reveal themselves, they can only be caught and put away so they can no longer harm others.

Revenge was not the force that drove me. I don't believe in capital punishment, although I don't judge people who do. However, it seems to me that if I condemn the act of murder, capital punishment is just a ritualized form of the same violence. When people who disagree say to me, "Oh, just put yourself in the victim's place," or, "You'd feel differently if it was someone you knew," all I can say is, "I know. I know."

In 2012, I was in northeast Florida a lot, researching a book about ghost lore and southern history. In a tourist shop on King Street, in St. Augustine, I picked up a copy of a paperback book. On the front cover, a picture of a young woman with her head tilted back, obviously a model from the 1950s, smiled at some long-forgotten camera. The ominous backdrop of the ancient city glowered in the distance. The title was *Bloody Sunset in St. Augustine.*

Bloody Sunset is a book based on the true story of Athalia Ponsell Lindsley's murder, written and published by people in the newspaper trade. Since they lived in St. Augustine, the authors had access to information that couldn't exactly be proven but definitely added an interesting perspective to the crime. There was no index or bibliography, no personal interviews or documented quotes. But the book did give an insider's account of the atmosphere of St. Augustine, the gist of the case and the lives of the people involved.

Many people who head for the Sunshine State are unaware that murder is not unusual in Florida. It is a fact that murder rates in the South are higher than in any other region of the United States. Florida, in particular, has many cold case homicides.

There were similarities between Athalia's gruesome end and my own father's murder. Athalia's death occurred one year, one month and one day before my own father's demise. Both victims were murdered in a suburban neighborhood, toward the front of the house closest to the street. The houses in each neighborhood were close in proximity, yet most neighbors heard nothing. Both murders were disorderly and risky crimes of passion executed in the throes of uncontrollable rage. In both cases, local Florida police with no experience in crime scenes handled the initial discovery. And although police were certain they knew who was responsible, no one was ever convicted of either crime. Committed in the heat of passion, these crimes are cold cases relegated to obscure case files, or their evidence is lost, thrown out or scattered.

I do not mean to imply that the same person committed both crimes. Of course, there is no question that my father's murder and Athalia's murder were carried out by different people in different cities. Yet the similarity in the time frame, the circumstances, the crime scene and the outcome speaks of a certain pattern. I began to believe that I might gain insight about murder by investigating the crime against Athalia Ponsell Lindsley. In addition, an unknown assailant murdered Frances Bemis, Athalia's neighbor, in November 1974. Her case was unsolved as well. Were the crimes related?

I wrote a chapter in my book *Haunted St. Augustine and St. Johns County,* about Athalia. During my book talks at libraries in St. Johns County, the most animated discussions occurred when the image of her house on Marine Street was displayed on the screen. Everyone knew about the murder and wanted to speculate about it.

Athalia's death had evolved from a private tragedy into public history. Public history is real-life drama. The story was provocative. Plenty of St. Augustine residents remembered the murder of Athalia Ponsell Lindsley. It received full news coverage from the *St. Augustine Record* and Jacksonville's *Florida Times-Union* newspapers. On the Internet, there were still message boards, a Facebook site and numerous articles and blogs dedicated to Athalia's memory. Even a local television show, *City Confidential*, featured a program about the crime in 2000 called "The Politician and the Socialite." That was the most polite title from the headlines written about her death, which included this gem in the *St. Augustine Record*: "Obnoxious Victim Had No Shortage of Possible Killers."

It is clear that an indifferent or a negative public perception of the murder victim has a great deal to do with apprehending and convicting the murderer. In Athalia's murder, there was a clear element of misogyny in the crime itself. American justice for murder victims, and for women in particular, is problematic then and now. In Athalia's case, the main suspect was a respected and well-liked member of the community, a city manager and her next-door neighbor. Athalia, on the other hand, was considered a "Yankee" in St. Augustine, even though she'd lived in Jacksonville for two decades. She was also a forthright, opinionated and outspoken woman in an era when such qualities were mainly the province of men.

Justice is largely a matter of control and influence. Serving justice often depends on the perceived character and the social status of the victim. Penalties, charges, testimonies and trial procedures hinge on cultural protocol, gender and racial stereotypes and media slant. When a woman attempts to apply equitable social standards to her daily actions, as Athalia did, she may be punished. J.C. Campbell in her 2003 paper for the *American Journal of Public Health* stated, "Femicide, the homicide of women, is…the seventh leading cause of premature death among women overall." In the 1970s, when Athalia was murdered and traditional expectations of women were much more prevalent, such statistics were not even measured.

Last, when I read *Bloody Sunset*, I was struck by the epilogue. Authors Mast and Powell wrote, "The story of the grisly hacking death of Athalia Lindsley remains unfinished because those who know the truth have remained silent all these years. One purpose of this book has been to present all the known pieces to the puzzle in a fashion that would stimulate interest in helping to find the missing parts."

"The missing parts." When someone is murdered, the bonds between remaining family members are rent and splintered, and often the familial relationship can never be put back together. Memories are tainted by horror. Athalia had no surviving children, her family was scattered and she had yet to reach her professional prime, despite the way the media characterized her

Number 124 Marine Street. *Photo by Bob Randall.*

as a washed-up showgirl. Didn't Athalia deserve to be remembered as the woman she really was?

A personal tragedy shaped my own life. It occurred to me that a fact-based book written about Athalia's death would be of benefit in understanding how murder—how all murders—evolve from a seemingly senseless pattern of prior events. So, over a period of several months, I read through more than one thousand pages of depositions, police reports and evidence. I traveled to St. Augustine, Florida; Charleston, South Carolina; and Northampton, Massachusetts, to pursue evidence, interviews and background. And I believe I came to understand how Athalia's murder happened, why it happened and what happened at about 6:00 p.m. on January 23, 1974, on the front steps of 124 Marine Street.

For me, and for others like me, understanding is the only road to peace.

ACKNOWLEDGEMENTS

Many people graciously assisted with filling in the gaps between 1974 and 2015, in many cases offering their valuable perspective. These good citizens include Dominic Nicklo, retired sergeant and first-class detective of the St. Augustine City Police; Carlton Moore, St. Johns County director of records; Sergeant Robert Dean of the St. Johns County Sheriff's Office and cold cases; Adrean King, St. Johns County evidence clerk; Stephanie Eliot, St. Johns County crime scene technician; Lieutenant Becky Clark, St. Johns County Sheriff's Office special projects manager at the Neil J. Perry Criminal Justice Facility; Kathleen Banks Nutter, archivist at the Sophia Smith Collection at Smith College; Anne Heymen, retired reporter at the *St. Augustine Record*; Philip Whitley, retired photographer at the *St. Augustine Record*; Delinda Fogel, publisher of the *St. Augustine Record*; Robert Duncan, operations manager at the Charleston County Clerk of Court; Sally Boyles, widow of State Attorney Stephen Boyles; Jim Mast, coauthor of *Bloody Sunset*; and Jean Troemel, former neighbor of Frances Bemis.

As always, thanks to my loving husband, Bob; to my daughter, Courtney; and to my granddaughter, Cassidy.

Introduction

A BRIEF HISTORY OF
ST. AUGUSTINE

The nature of history is to synthesize. Told from a variety of perspectives, it is the historian's job to nail down facts and to provide context. Athalia Ponsell Lindsley's murder did not occur randomly, nor did it occupy a figurative vacuum in time. For this reason, perspective and a brief history of the city of St. Augustine is warranted, not only as a record of human behavior but also to quantify human nature, if such a thing is possible.

One common characteristic that all human beings share are our stories— stories we tell ourselves and stories we tell about one another. Narratives are how people understand their environments. Joseph Campbell, author of *The Hero with a Thousand Faces*, wrote, "Myths are public dreams, dreams are private myths." Like many prominent cities, the history of St. Augustine begins with a myth. Students learn that Juan Ponce de León landed in 1513 on the coast of St. Augustine and bequeathed the name *La Florida* to this veritable land of flowers. In truth, Ponce de León's famous discovery of Florida probably did not occur in St. Augustine. It is more likely that the diminutive explorer, lauded in a statue near the Bridge of Lions, landed nearer to Melbourne, Florida. His search for the Fountain of Youth was a myth as well. Yet even without Ponce de León's presence, St. Augustine does enjoy status as America's oldest continuously occupied European settlement. It had been around for twenty years when the English colonists of Roanoke settled in Virginia. It was there forty-two years before Jamestown and fifty-five years

Ponce de Leon.

Kapitel VIII.

Florida;

Historic illustration of Ponce de Leon. *Courtesy of the Library of Congress.*

before the Pilgrims landed in Plymouth.

The true origins of the city began with an order by King Phillip II to secure the coastal property he had already claimed from the heathen French Huguenots. Pedro Menéndez de Avilés, the Spanish king's admiral, first sighted land on August 28, 1565, the feast day of St. Augustine. He named the city after his saintly mentor and dispatched the French Huguenots near the Matanzas River (the Spanish word for slaughter is *matanzas*) in a bloody execution after they were shipwrecked during a hurricane. Tourists can see the approximate spot of the Huguenot massacre from the nature trail at Fort Matanzas National Park. There's a stone marker that reads, in all caps, "MASSACRE BY MENENDEZ OF RIBAULT AND HIS MEN, SEPTEMBER 1565." Near that date, the admiral also attended a holy mass at what is now the shrine of La Leche. Since 1965, St. Augustine celebrates this event every fifty years with fireworks, entertainment, foreign dignitaries and tourist currency flowing into city coffers.

In keeping with its bloody origin, St. Augustine's history, like most American settlements, was marked by disease, conflict and peril. It was little more than a fortress for many years and used as a base for far-flung Catholic missions. It burned to the ground more than once. The sovereign flag of St. Augustine switched back and forth between Spain and England and back again to Spain before the United States hoisted the Stars and Stripes in 1821. That year, St. Augustine suffered the worst outbreak of yellow fever in its history. A "public" cemetery was opened to accommodate all the victims.

Marker on Fort Matanzas of Huguenot slaughter by Pedro Menéndez. *Photo by Bob Randall.*

According to Florence S. Mitchell's book *A History of the Huguenot Cemetery*, thirteen or fourteen people, including soldiers, were dying every day.

Its territorial standing under the United States in the 1830s did not prevent bitter rancor between Indians and nonnative Americans in St. Augustine

Left: Huguenot Cemetery. *Photo by Bob Randall.*

Below: Outer wall of Castillo de San Marcos. *Photo by Bob Randall.*

during the Seminole Indian Wars. The "half-breed" Chief Osceola was a prisoner in the dungeon of the Castillo de San Marcos before being transferred to Fort Moultrie in South Carolina, where he died. Ghost tours declare that Chief Osceola's suffering face is still visible on the outer wall of the fort above the dry moat.

By the time the Civil War rolled around, Union and Confederate sympathies were deeply divided. Even though the city fell to Union troops, culturally, St. Augustine remains a deeply southern town. A number of English residents who lived there for generations were accustomed to the insular privileges of aristocracy. Outsiders included Yankees, blacks, Indians

Waterfront in St. Augustine during the Civil War era. *Courtesy of the Library of Congress.*

and just about anyone whose family hadn't been born generations ago in cities like St. Augustine, Atlanta, Memphis, Richmond, Savannah or Charleston. A former resident of the oldest city declared, "The caste system in St. Augustine was more rigid than India's. If you're not an insider, you're locked out. There was no New Guard. The Old Guard reproduced."

By the turn of the twentieth century, Jim Crow laws also characterized the city. Thus, during the civil rights movement in the 1960s, the established and privileged citizens of St. Augustine believed that society functioned best when everything—and everyone—was in its place. They believed that there were no racial issues in St. Augustine. They saw themselves as rational about change, which they saw no need to accelerate. The problems that ensued resulted not only from the fact that they were wrong—anyone can be wrong—but also because they gave implicit support to aggression, supporting their erroneous beliefs.

Anyone who challenged the status quo was labeled a problem. Organizations such as the National Association for the Advancement of Colored People (NAACP) and the Southern Christian Leadership Conference (SCLC) were labeled a problem. Martin Luther King Jr., who famously visited the city to rally civil rights supporters in 1964, was labeled a problem. He was arrested and spent the night in the St. Augustine jail along with countless other foot soldiers of the civil rights movement.

But that wasn't the worst of it. When a federal district judge, Bryon Simpson (an old chum of prominent Jacksonville defense lawyer Walter Arnold, who is portrayed in this book), demanded that city leaders abandon an imposed curfew and allow civil rights demonstrations to continue as their First Amendment rights dictated, city leaders howled that federal courts had taken over their jurisdiction. The *St. Augustine Record* published their comments.

In fact, it is well documented that during the civil rights movement, St. Johns County city leadership—in the form of the religious leaders, the business guild, the mayor, the governor, the sheriff, the chief of police and the commissioners—distinguished themselves by abandoning law and order to notorious white supremacists. At the height of the turmoil, the leader of the local integrationists, a dentist named Robert Hayling, was viciously beaten and almost killed during a Klan meeting in 1963. Dr. Hayling was consequently hospitalized and charged with assault.

Yet even after the passage of the Civil Rights Act in 1964, many businesses, educational institutions, religious facilities and municipal organizations in St. Augustine had to be forced to enact equitable access and support the civil rights of their black citizens. And many of these city leaders and decision

Foot soldiers of the civil rights movement. *Photo by Bob Randall.*

makers during the racial turmoil of St. Augustine in the 1960s were still around ten years later in one role or another in the aftermath of the Athalia Ponsell Lindsley murder.

In fact, these men—the elite, the city leaders—knew one another very well. Perhaps it is only natural that their communal association in the Episcopalian Church, the St. Augustine Chamber of Commerce, the St. Augustine Historical Society, the Country Club, the Rotary Club, Toastmasters, the Elks, the Kiwanis and the Knights of Pythias supplemented the already entwined nature of their interactions. Their main objectives were the status quo, fraternity and the protection of their business and political interests. And into this paternalistic stew, where everyone knew his or her place, dropped Athalia Ponsell in 1971.

Athalia was no integrationist, but she was still an outsider. She presented a different perspective and a different persona than the typical middle-aged dowager. And in spite of her work history as a Powers model, she was not the type of woman to sit down, shut up and smile.

Athalia was, quite definitely, a problem.

DEATH BEFORE DUSK

I kissed her and said, "I'll see you in an hour."
–James "Jinx" Lindsley

Note: The reader will note that the times recorded for events are inconsistent, but these are based on the original documentation.

On January 23, 1974, it was a Wednesday, under the astrological sign of Aquarius. Richard Nixon was president, and he moved to enhance oil production in the United States by giving tax breaks to American oil companies and by scaling back clean air laws. The national headlines were full of news about Watergate, the energy crisis, the Kissinger-negotiated Israeli troop pullback from Cairo and space exploration vis-à-vis Apollo 14. A new movie with Robert Redford, *The Sting*, was out, and the top two songs in the United States were Streisand's "The Way We Were" and Miller's "The Joker."

On January 23, 1974, news in the *St. Augustine Record* (masthead motto: "Serving St. Johns County and the nation's oldest city since 1894") focused on continuing efforts of Flagler College to receive accreditation and on the formation of the Historic Architectural Review Board to oversee new construction governing historic districts. Local news focused on the recent county commission meeting. Frank Upchurch Jr., a lawyer, was honored by the Kiwanis. Two high school students, Hunter Barnett and James McAdams, were honored by the Elks Lodge. In a letter to the editor titled

The *St. Augustine Record. Photo by Bob Randall.*

"A Certain Spirit of Care," Merri Vale Ormond wrote, "What a wonderful town St. Augustine is."

On January 23, 1974, in St. Augustine, Florida, the barometric pressure was 30.18, with a relative humidity of 70 percent. It was foggy that morning and cool, but by 6:00 p.m., the temperature was a perfect seventy-two degrees. The sun wouldn't set until 6:55 p.m. since Florida skipped daylight savings time that year, and full dark would not descend until 8:17 p.m. Fog was likely.

The view from the house on 124 Marine Street faced the Matanzas Bay, but it did not provide a full sunset because it did not face the west. However, the woman lying sprawled on the front steps of her white mansion was beyond caring. Her head, attached by a single sinewy thread to the rest of her body, rested on the bottom step of the front porch. She stared at nothing with wide-open eyes and an almost benign expression, which belied the sprawled, "broken doll" appearance of the rest of her body. And the blood. Blood pooled everywhere, as it does when the carotid artery is severed. Blood was also splattered all over the east wall of the home.

The woman's blue and white dress was hiked up, and she'd lost a shoe. Her pearls were scattered on the sidewalk. Some of her fingers were severed, and there were defensive wounds on her arms. For the moment, she was alone, but heads were starting to turn in her direction, just as they always had throughout her life. Athalia Ponsell Lindsley was not a woman to ignore. And now, for one last time, she was the complete center of attention.

Marine Street was near Flagler Hospital, and it was a busy road even on its best days. At 5:59 p.m. (documented time), Mr. Quentin Odell was on his way to Flagler Hospital to pick up his daughter. He passed a yellow car on Marine Street coming the other way, driving slowly past the Lindsley home, driving the way people do when there's been an accident, as though the people in the car were looking at something.

The Meirs, a local couple, drove right by the house and then doubled back when they realized what they'd seen. What they didn't see was anyone else walking down the street.

But Mr. B.O. Brunson of 101 Marine Street reported sitting on the front steps of his house at 5:50 p.m. (documented time) when a man drove up in a white Volkswagen. "Call an ambulance and the police department," the man said. "A woman has fallen out of a window, there's blood all over the place."

A few minutes earlier, Patti Stanford of 126 Marine Street was at the sink rinsing dishes. She looked out the window and then hustled her daughter Patricia into the hall of the home and handed her the baby of the family, three-year-old Annette. Patti said, "You take the baby and do something with her." At that moment, they both heard their neighbor Rosemary McCormick screaming, "Alan, Patti, come here quick!"

Neighbors to the north and south of 124 Marine Street, Rosemary McCormick and Patti Stanford, met briefly at the wrought-iron link fence on the edge of the lawn of 124 Marine Street, holding their hands to their mouths. "I wish I hadn't looked," Patti said.

By 6:08 p.m. (documented time), Rosemary's son, Locke, had called the police and an ambulance. Approximately thirty seconds later, an ambulance drove by heading toward the accident/crime scene. A few minutes later, Patti Stanford's daughter Patricia took her baby sister, Annette, upstairs. Patricia stared out her bedroom window. Annette played at Patricia's feet.

Patricia had a view into the part of the National Guard Cemetery where children played hide-and-seek among the tombstones on sunny winter days like that one. In the other direction, she could see into the McCormicks' yard. Short of that and right next door, she could see the front stoop of

Ambulance and police on Marine Street. *Courtesy of Philip Whitley and the* St. Augustine Record.

the Lindsley house. She saw "Mrs. Lindsley laying on the front steps." Mrs. Lindsley was covered with blood.

Athalia's husband, James Lindsley, arrived at his home on Lew Street a few minutes before 6:00 p.m. He and Athalia were still newlyweds, and they'd had trouble selling her house on Marine Street. As they were both seasoned real estate agents, they'd taken it off the market for a while and planned to try again in the spring. In the meantime, Athalia's pets still lived there, and she spent time there, too, tending to them and guarding thirty years of possessions.

So, at 5:30 p.m., James kissed Athalia outside his real estate office on St. George Street and said, "I'll see you in an hour." When he arrived home, he took the groceries inside that he and Athalia had picked up during their leisurely day together in Jacksonville. James and Athalia were celebrating the Chinese New Year that night, and the groceries were snow peas, water chestnuts and bamboo shoots, items unavailable in St. Augustine grocery stores and items James would be eating alone in the days to come.

Earlier that day, during lunch, Athalia warned her husband, whose nickname was "Jinx," that according to an old Chinese custom it was bad luck to use knives on the Chinese New Year. She cut her fish with her fork.

After he unpacked the groceries, James "got some clothes off," changed into jeans, took off his shirt and called Athalia's number on the phone. She'd said she'd be right over after she unpacked her half of the groceries and took care of the pets. His newspaper hadn't come that day, so he wanted her to bring one so he could check on any news about Athalia's appearance the day before at a commission meeting. He called again and received no answer. He wasn't alarmed. "I thought she was out in the yard," he said.

James went outside because he had "two hoses dribbling all the time." He moved them to different shrubberies. When he came in, he watched the news. At about 6:30 p.m., the phone rang. It was Esther Stucky from Riberia Street. She said, "Jim, get over to Athalia's, something awful has happened. There are police all around the house."

"What is it?" asked James.

"Just get over there." Mrs. Stucky rang off.

James changed his pants, put his shirt on and started out the door. The phone rang again. It was Jean Troemel, a local artist and one of Athalia's neighbors. She said, "Jim, you better get over there, there is a big crowd around Athalia's. I don't know what happened, but it must be something bad." James never admitted that he made one phone call before he left home. Yet his lawyer, Robbie Andreu, was there by the time James arrived at the Marine Street house.

Over on Chapel Street, Sergeant Dominic Nicklo, a detective for the City of St. Augustine, had just gotten off work and walked into his home at 6:35 p.m. (documented time). The telephone began ringing. It was the police station dispatcher summoning him to the crime scene.

And so, one by one, in groups, in pairs, on foot and in vehicles, St. Augustine residents, ambulance attendants, police and detectives gathered to stare, gawk, investigate, surmise, speculate and, for some, grieve. Athalia's dull eyes, her broken body, her life's blood lay under the drifting clouds of a blue sky. Chief of Police Virgil Stuart declared that Athalia's murder was "a crime of just pure hate.... She was dead when we got there.... She had been badly butchered. Her head was almost cut off."

Forty years later, a study by Cardiff University in Wales determined that January 23, for one reason or another, is the saddest day of the year.

THE CRIME SCENE

My wife had no enemies—except one.
—James "Jinx" Lindsley

It was reported as a "domestic going on." Officers Larrow and Janson were the first police representatives on the scene at 124 Marine Street. Associated Ambulance attendants James Rousseau and Ron Nabors met them on the front steps. Athalia Ponsell Lindsley's body was still on the sidewalk covered with a reddening sheet. It was reported that death was "probably caused by a sharp instrument, which struck the victim a number of times about the head, face, arms, and hands." No murder weapon was found.

Officer Francis O'Loughlin arrived, and he and Officer Joe Larrow walked into the house, where they left at least one bloody footprint. No one was in the house, and nothing seemed to be disturbed. They found Athalia's bag of groceries, upright and unspilled, on the kitchen floor. The back door, which led through the kitchen, was closed, but Athalia's keys still dangled from the lock. Her niece, Patricia Tilson from Virginia, would say later that her aunt "was very precise in keeping her doors and windows locked. She would not have gone outside to talk to a stranger."

The men went back outside. Rousseau and Nabors said they hadn't seen anyone in the area when they arrived. Officer Larrow decided to go next door to interview Locke McCormick, who'd called the police and the ambulance. Locke, Athalia's eighteen-year-old next-door neighbor, was home from his Daytona Beach college to help with a local high school play.

Athalia's corpse covered with a sheet in front of her blood-splattered house. *Courtesy of Philip Whitley and the* St. Augustine Record.

Groceries on the floor. *Courtesy of Philip Whitley and the* St. Augustine Record.

Keys in the lock. *Courtesy of Philip Whitley and the* St. Augustine Record.

Locke grew up in St. Augustine on Marine Street. His grandmother Mrs. Claude Smith lived across the street, and before Athalia's mother bought the house, Locke's best friend lived right next door. He was a happy kid who rode his bike all summer long, liked to play poker and took advanced classes at St. Augustine High School. Locke was a quintessential local boy whom former classmates described as "the nicest kid ever." He was, as it turned out, the only eyewitness to come forward regarding Athalia's murder.

Locke told the officers that around 6:10 p.m. (documented time), his mother was in the kitchen, and he was sitting on the couch in the den of his house, watching TV, when he heard "loud snapping sounds" like "hands clapping." He got up and looked out the window, which faced the Lindsley home. He saw a white man wearing a white dress shirt and dark pants standing with his back to the McCormick home in front of the steps of the

Lindsley home. The man's hair was brown, gray and closely trimmed. Locke yelled something to his mother and ran outside.

About eight to ten feet from the doorstep, he saw the man's shoulder moving up and down as though he were "swinging an object out of Locke's view." The clapping sounds stopped. Then the man began walking slowly south from the Lindsley home and "angle[d] off" in a southwesterly direction out of his sight. Locke took a few steps forward. He saw Athalia's body. He ran into his house and yelled, "Call the police! No! Call an ambulance first!"

The police asked him if the man held anything in his hands. Locke said, "I didn't notice." That may have been because he was still distracted. Locke didn't mention the initial screams, but Patti Stanford, standing at her sink rinsing supper dishes, heard them. At first she thought, "Somebody got run over. We have such a busy street; the cars go so fast out there." Her eighteen-year-old daughter, Patricia, thought the screams were "little kids down the street that are always screaming." They were both wrong.

Athalia died "almost instantly" according to the autopsy performed later by coroner Dr. Albert Schwartz in Daytona Beach. So, after her death throes, the consequent screams were from her neighbors Rosemary McCormick and Patti Stanford. Patti remained "hysterical" then and for far into the evening, according to a neighbor, Mrs. Genie Dodds, from Charlotte Street.

Meanwhile, at least six other police officers arrived, including Sergeant Nicklo, who traced a trail of blood "going from the body over to the wall separating the Lindsley house from the Stanford house."

The *St. Augustine Record*'s chief photographer, Philip Whitley, "got the call" and was taking pictures. "People were walking through the yard and climbing over hedges," he said. "The whole thing was a screwed up mess from beginning to end. They were destroying the crime scene." He, too, saw blood in the grass, "leading all around the south side of the house." At one point, he said, one of the police officers ordered the ambulance attendants to hose down the blood "where it was concentrated to the left of the front door and at the bottom of the steps."

There was gossip later that washing away some of the blood evidence was deliberate and that it was done to protect James Lindsley, who was immediately one of the main suspects. James was a good ol' boy, a former mayor and a county commissioner, born and bred in St. Augustine. Dudley Garrett, whom James supported in a successful run for sheriff, was called, although the city police were already there.

Meanwhile, Whitley went over to the McCormicks' to see his good friend, Assistant State Attorney Richard O. Watson, who would later work for the prosecution of the murder case. Colonel Connie McCormick was away in

Alan's county ride. *Courtesy of the St. Johns County Sheriff's Department.*

Mexico on a hunting trip, so Watson was talking to Rosemary and Locke and just generally seething. "Watson," Whitley said, "was a smart man, fair as he could be and a good person. But he was having a fit about how the police were handling the case. But they'd never had anything like that. Just shootings, stabbings in bars."

Sergeant Nicklo independently concurred. "Law enforcement then," he said, "is not what it is today. There is so much forensic evidence now. Then we didn't even have our own crime scene unit. You had to call Jacksonville FDLE [Florida Department of Law Enforcement], which is what the sheriff did, to bring their crime scene unit down."

Around 7:00 p.m., Mr. Alan G. Stanford Jr., Athalia's next-door neighbor on the south side, pulled up into the driveway of his home. He was in a 1970 Chevy Impala, a car with a county seal, a perk he was entitled to as county manager of St. Johns County. His office was in a huge corrugated tin structure called the Road and Bridge Building off County Road 16. When St. Augustine city police told him his neighbor was dead, Stanford asked, "Was she shot or was she cut?"

Left out of the police report was what Locke screamed to his mother as he witnessed Athalia's death. Later, he told Hoopie Tebault, editor of the *St. Augustine Record*, the same thing: "Mr. Stanford was hitting Mrs. Ponsell."

THE UNUSUAL AND THE
USUAL SUSPECTS

The trail is cold. I doubt we'll ever catch the killer.
—St. Augustine police chief Virgil Stuart

It is likely that no one felt safe in St. Augustine after the event of January 23, 1974. However, St. Johns County citizens kept up a brave front. Frances Bemis, a resident on Marine Street and an acquaintance of Athalia's quoted in the *Record*, said, "I think St. Augustine is the safest place I've ever lived in. The people here are wonderful. I go out walking at night and will continue to do so. I went out walking the same night the murder took place. I see people walking their dogs every night."

This laissez-faire attitude did not extend to local law enforcement. One of the complaints of Walter Arnold, the attorney in charge of defense in the consequent murder trial, was that the police settled on one suspect and did not look hard enough for the true culprit. He complained, "We received nothing as to any other investigation other than as it reflects directly on my client." However, extensive police records, which exist to this day, prove that Arnold's accusation was incorrect, that there was plenty of follow-up and plenty of documentation and that it was no secret.

The police made many mistakes in pursing Athalia's murderer: at the crime scene, with the search warrant, during the collection of evidence and in providing pivotal law enforcement officials to testify at the trial. But they also did many things right in spite of their inexperience with capital murder offenses. There are close to one thousand pages of interviews, depositions, evidence and notes regarding their keen pursuit of justice in Athalia's murder case—justice they were under no community pressure to provide.

In life, Athalia could be intimidating, aggressive and single minded—qualities that were abhorred in women, especially in southern society in the 1970s. Many citizens of the city thought that she was "a troublemaker" and were not sorry that she was permanently gone. Francis O'Loughlin, one of the first officers on the scene, said, "I will always remember the remarks made by some that the woman had earned her own death."

Sally Boyles, the widow of former state attorney Steven Boyles, said, "Not that St. Augustine citizens went around killing people they didn't like. But Athalia was not on a level playing field. Nobody liked her, so there was not a big hue and cry when she was killed."

Regardless, law enforcement in St. Johns County rallied to the task of finding Athalia's killer. Although the St. Augustine PD were the first officers on the scene, the St. Johns County Sheriff's Office became involved the evening of the murder when Sheriff Garret showed up at 8:00 p.m. (documented time). Two of his officers—Lieutenant Eddie Lightsey and Captain Robert Williams were in Orlando attending, ironically, a seminar on forensic evidence in homicide. But they were back before noon the next day, and both assumed leadership roles in assembling evidence and in interviewing potential witnesses.

"It started out the city would work the case," said Sergeant Nicklo, "but it became a dual investigation with the city and the sheriff's office. The Sheriff had the most authority, but we just kind of melded together. And, at the Sheriff's request, FDLE brought Special Agent Dallas Herring in too."

Sheriff Dudley W. Garrett Jr. deserves the most credit for his leadership in the thoroughness of the murder investigation. He launched "a street by street sweep" of the city. A team of deputies and police officers interviewed hundreds of people and documented it even if the report noted that the interviewee "did not hear or see anything unusual." He corresponded with local and distant agencies probing similarities in recent crimes. Garrett did not believe that "the slaying could have happened without arousing some suspicion by neighbors, passersby, or others." The sheriff worked systematically, eliminating information in order to allow real clues and real suspects to emerge.

For example, the St. Johns County Sheriff's Office determined quickly that the murder weapon was a machete "because of the depths of the cuts." According to Captain Williams in his June 20 deposition, "They were real clean cuts as they went in…just as clean like you had taken a razor. And long."

The outer focus of Garrett's investigation included anyone arrested with a machete in his possession. This, actually, allowed for a wide range of suspects. As Walter Arnold stated in his autobiography, *Not Guilty*, "nearly all the residents of St. Johns County owned one or two machetes for trimming palm fronds and cutting vines and bushes."

Nevertheless, Garrett was making sure. There was a Daytona Beach man, Gary Powell, held in the Duval County jail on charges of robbery and possession of a controlled substance. He was arrested with a "meat cleaver-type cutting instrument in his automobile." Garrett sent Special Agent Herring to Jacksonville to interview Powell.

Sheriff Garrett, Officer Nicklo and Officer Davis traveled to the Daytona Beach Police Department to meet with Detective J.H. Jenkins to investigate another white male, Thad Rutkowski, who was found with a "machete-type knife" on him after being charged with the robbery of a hotel.

In another scenario, a neighbor, Elizabeth Williams, relayed a story that Athalia told her about a "businessman in Cuba who garroted his secretary," and the report was duly documented by Lieutenant Lightsey. There is even correspondence from Sheriff Garrett and Police Chief Virgil Stuart that indicated the murder investigation extended to Los Angeles, California.

Even rumors were investigated. An article in the *Florida Times-Union* by Dick Hagood on February 1, 1974, mentioned a "bushy-haired Oriental" who was spotted by an unknown witness leaving the scene of the Marine Street crime.

By far, the most time spent on a dead end occurred with twenty-year-old Adelle McLoughlin, who, as she rode her bicycle down Marine Street, claimed to have seen a "white man in his late 50s opening the gate to the driveway" of Athalia's house about 4:30 p.m. on the day of the murder.

None of these suspects panned out. Powell knew no one in St. Augustine. Rutkowski was mentally ill and had no transportation. The mysterious Cuban never materialized. There were no viable leads from California. No one ever admitted seeing the Asian man with the wild hair. Adelle McLoughlin turned out to be the daughter of a man who worked for Alan Stanford, a man with a stake in establishing alternate suspects. She may have seen someone near Athalia's house, but Marine Street was a busy thoroughfare for traffic and pedestrians and it could have been anyone.

As James Lindsley said, "This town has been hip deep in rumors with every kind of crazy goddamn story you can think of. Hell, I've been under suspicion and I don't know who else hasn't." This was true. But right from the start, as Captain Williams admitted in his deposition, there were two main suspects.

The first, in fact, was Athalia's husband, James "Jinx" Lindsley. In spite of James being a St. Augustine insider, a former mayor and a commissioner, he was described as a chain smoker who drank too much by those who knew him and as "abrasive" by everyone else. And he wasn't nicknamed "Jinx" for nothing. He'd been married twice before to the same woman, a dance instructor named Lillian. They had a son, Danny, who died in a motorcycle accident in 1966. Lillian died on New Year's Day 1971 in the early morning hours in a car crash near the Duval County line, with James at the wheel. At the age of sixty, her neck was broken from the impact of the crash. No breathalyzer test or blood alcohol analysis was taken of either party in the accident.

Much was made of the fact that James and Athalia married after dating only a few months in 1973. Then they maintained separate residences. Certainly, she stayed at the house on 124 Marine Street to safeguard her possessions. Yet it soon emerged that there were indeed marital difficulties between the newlyweds.

Athalia confided in a letter to her sister, Geraldine Horton of Honolulu, that James was "a leech" and "a liar." Once, when Athalia asked James to mail a letter with a fifty-dollar check inside, James removed the check and cashed it. Athalia told her sister that she, Geraldine, and Geraldine's daughter, Patricia, were the beneficiaries of her will and that James should receive nothing. She made it clear that James did not even have a key to her house on Marine Street.

As bad as that sounds, it does not take into account how difficult it is to pool resources and lifestyles in a mature marriage. Athalia was fifty-six when she and James were wed on September 10, 1973, and he was sixty-four. Athalia's mother died in April after a lengthy illness, and Athalia was her caretaker. James had just lost an election to the county commission, his first election defeat in more than a decade. They both had recent traumatic life-changing events in common. It made sense to consolidate their assets.

They were both realtors—in fact, that was how they met—but the 1970s was a bad time for real estate. Mortgage interest rates spiked at 9 percent, and they would peak as high as 22 percent by the early '80s. It was hard to sell Athalia's big, expensive house. In addition, Athalia was naturally protective of her mother's valuable possessions at the Marine Street home. She kept her dogs there, a crippled bird and, at one time, according to records, a goat. Athalia was a divorced woman unaccustomed to sharing time or resources. Athalia had not entirely

Lindsley house, 1930s. *Courtesy of the Library of Congress.*

coordinated her routines or her habits with James in spite of their recent marriage. But she was trying.

At least one neighbor, Frances Bemis, wrote to Sheriff Garrett about the "great affection" the pair exhibited when they were together and that she was sure they had "a good relationship." Even Athalia's sister, Geraldine, asserted that Athalia did not talk much about "any difficulty she was having with James Lindsley." And James Lindsley was unmistakably besotted with Athalia. "I loved her so," he said later. "We were together almost every hour of the day except at night when she went home to her house." But James was used to that. He and his first wife, Lillian, always owned two homes, sometimes stayed together and sometimes stayed in separate residences.

Athalia accompanied James to his real estate office at 214 St. George Street almost every day. It was a historic building, one of the oldest in St. Augustine, and rumored to be haunted. On January 23, as they did at least once a week, Athalia and James skipped work and spent a companionable day together taking a shopping trip to Jacksonville. They drove to Jacksonville in James's newish green Pinto wagon because he felt it was more reliable than Athalia's 1957 Cadillac sedan. James gave Athalia twenty dollars and dropped her off at Levy-Wolf's, a department store, while he went to a brokerage office across the street. Athalia bought James a shirt, some underwear and socks; looked at some shoes; and picked up a repaired necklace from Wells Jewelers. They met in front of Morrison's restaurant across from Hemming Park at 3:30 p.m. when the stock market closed. Then they shopped for their groceries for their Chinese dinner and headed home.

Athalia was seen leaving James's real estate office on 214 St. George Street at about 5:35 p.m. (documented time). She was going home to feed her dogs and to allow her crippled pet blue jay, Clementine, some exercise on her front lawn, as she customarily did. Then she planned to pick up the mail and the paper, close the blinds, turn on a light and the radio to make it look as though someone were home, lock up tight and head over to James's house at 955 Lew Boulevard on Anastasia Island, on the other side of the Bridge of Lions.

After Athalia left for home, James walked back to his office to see if he had any messages on his "recorder." He locked up the office and got back into his car. A Mrs. Fagen saw him leave. So did Mrs. Ruth Parker, a manager of a dress shop on King Street, who was walking to her car.

From there, he went through the parking lot to Cordova Street and parked in front of McCartney's Drugstore on King Street. Before he entered, he ran into the Upchurch brothers, Hamilton and Frank Jr., and he spoke with them for a few minutes. Then he talked to a friend from his real estate business, Charles Benninger, before he went into the drugstore to buy some cough drops. A Mr. Robert Osbourne stated that he saw the Lindsley car in front of the drugstore at about 5:30 p.m. (documented time).

After James left, he drove over the Bridge of Lions and onto Anastasia Boulevard, where he stopped by Skinner's Dairy to get some milk. When he arrived home, at about 6:05 p.m. (documented time), he saw his neighbor Mr. Best about fifty feet away. The two men did not speak, but Mr. Ronald Best confirmed later to Sergeant Dominic Nicklo that he saw James arrive in the Lindsley car port near the front door between 6:00 p.m. and 6:30 p.m. (documented time).

Special Agent Dallas Herring was concerned that "there was a time lapse of approximately 15 to 25 minutes which were unaccounted for in Lindsley's alibi." Presumably this lapse occurred during his drive home from McCartney's, although it is a stretch to presume that he could have made it to Marine Street, hacked his wife to death and returned to his home on Lew Street by 6:05 p.m. On February 5, Special Agent Dallas Herring arranged for James Lindsley to take a lie detector test administered by a polygraph examiner, Special Agent Joe Townsend, also of the FDLE, Tallahassee field office. Lindsley passed the polygraph test, and Townsend declared that James Lindsley "was truthful about his knowledge of events surrounding the death of his wife."

Lindsley said, "It's a terrible, terrible thing not only to have such a grievous loss, but also to have those invisible fingers of suspicion pointing at you. At least this has taken some of the weight off my mind, although it doesn't take any of the sorrow away."

Clearly, James's account of his whereabouts on January 23 was solid. For one thing, it never varied. For another, it is impossible that so many unrelated people who saw James Lindsley in town and at his home around the approximate time of his wife's murder could have conspired together to provide him with an alibi. In fact, Frank Upchurch Jr. was hired within a month to provide a defense for another, much more viable suspect.

This particular suspect was someone with whom Athalia had an ongoing feud. This suspect allegedly threatened her life. This suspect's alibi timeline changed continually, and his home was where the trail of blood leading from Athalia's house ended. This suspect borrowed a machete from the county and never returned it. This suspect was initially identified as the killer by Locke McCormick, who was the only eyewitness who came forward.

He was the most logical suspect, and he was also the county manager, a vestryman at Trinity Episcopal Church, a husband, a father and Athalia's next-door neighbor. He was Alan Griffith Stanford Jr.

THE DISPUTE

Your wife was meddling in my business with the dogs last fall.
—Athalia Ponsell Lindsley

Marine Street was not a neighborhood prone to friendly garage sales, block parties or potluck suppers. Frances Bemis, Athalia's neighbor on Marine Street, created and chaired a committee in the late 1950s "to create a warmer, friendlier and more hospitable atmosphere in our lovely community...too many people go elsewhere after trying us out...we must bring newcomers and older residents together." Frances held meetings at the mayor's house, obtained lists of new residents from real estate agents and planned social events. Unfortunately, when she resigned as chairwoman, no one took up the mantle. By the 1970s, Frances's efforts to welcome new homeowners had been over for sixteen years.

It seems that no one welcomed Athalia Ponsell Lindsley and her mother, Margherita Fetter, when they established residency at the Marine Street house. Since neighborly contact was at a minimum, it was difficult to determine how the dispute between Athalia and her neighbors on both sides of her house began. There are many missing pieces to the narrative, most notably Athalia's voice. History only reveals her reaction and not the entire story of what motivated it.

It began with Athalia's barking dogs. The houses on Marine Street were close together, and the basic St. Augustine yard was devoid of lush landscapes. There were chain link fences enclosing the front yards and crabgrass, palmettos and banana trees in the rear. There were no bushes in between the houses. Proximity was not always kind, and Athalia was the subject of gossip and speculation right from the start. Mrs. Smith, Mrs. McCormick and Mrs. Stanford joked together about the pink wraparound that Athalia wore in her yard some mornings when she gardened. Clearly, they commiserated about Athalia's seven dogs, which "barked, fought and howled" at all hours of the day and night. The McCormicks and Patti Stanford even went so far as to file a public complaint against Athalia in October 1972, shortly after she moved in with her mother.

Athalia and her mother had moved to St. Augustine from Jacksonville, where they lived together in an "old mansion" on Riverside Avenue. Athalia's mother, Margherita Fetter, bought the house on Marine Street from a Mrs. Winnifred McCarter Shipman. However, it is likely that Athalia handled the transaction in lieu of her mother. Mrs. Fetter, a retired schoolteacher from Duval County and a widow since 1937, was an invalid. Geraldine Horton, Athalia's sister, mentioned flying home from Honolulu for her mother's "heart attacks." Athalia was her mother's caretaker for many years.

It is hard to understand why Athalia picked St. Augustine as the place she wanted to live. She and her mother were comfortable in Jacksonville. The Duval County Republican Women's Club president, Elinor Van Dyke, said, "Most of us knew Athalia well for a long period and loved her dearly." Perhaps Athalia wanted a fresh start in a city where she had fond girlhood memories; she and her sister, Geraldine, had attended the local St. Joseph Academy. Perhaps she thought St. Johns County was a smaller, more suitable venue in which to exercise her budding political ambition. Perhaps the upkeep of the mansion on Riverside was too expensive.

Whatever the reason, Athalia was probably shocked by her reception in the St. Augustine community. There were no covered casseroles or home-baked cookies to welcome her to the neighborhood. Frances Bemis's committee to greet newcomers was long gone. Instead, the complaint about Athalia's barking dogs "on one of the best streets" in St. Augustine began.

It's not as though all was peace and quiet before she came. Marine Street was a busy thoroughfare in those days, and there was always the sound of traffic. The hospital was at one end, and the sound of ambulance sirens and people driving back and forth kept up a steady stream of traffic noise. It is a mystery how the barking from Athalia's dogs was so disruptive to her neighbors and yet not disruptive to her or to the invalid in her own house. At least one of the dogs, Zsa Zsa, was quite old and had been Margherita's beloved pet for years.

As her mother's caretaker, Athalia was home all the time because her mother could not even go to the bathroom by herself. Clearly, Margherita Fetter, whose heart was bad, needed a lot of rest. At one point, Mrs. Fetter fell and broke her hip. If Athalia was at home, tending to the dogs and twenty-four-hour caretaking of her mother, how could the noise be that bad?

Yet why did Athalia take such umbrage when her neighbors complained about the noise? Reasonable people try to work things out. Athalia's sister, Geraldine, described Athalia as "a wonderful person taking care of people… she always helped." She was also not uncooperative. One of Athalia's neighbors, Elizabeth Williams, complained about the "outside lights in the backyard" of 124 Marine Street "shining in her window" at night. Shortly before Athalia was killed, Elizabeth knocked on Athalia's door after 10:00 p.m. and asked her to turn the floodlights off. Athalia politely did so, but Mrs. Williams observed that Athalia "appeared scared."

Geraldine noted during one of her visits to Athalia's house that the McCormicks "said something" when the dogs were in the yard, and Athalia responded in a temperate way: "Leave the dogs alone, please." Unfortunately, only the McCormicks' and the Stanfords' view of the dog dispute were documented, and they portrayed Athalia as a crazed vigilante. She was convicted of disturbing the peace and fined fifty dollars. Athalia did not show up in court, probably because she was taking care of her mother.

Consequently, she boarded all but three of her dogs, but her neighbors were still dissatisfied and reportedly still disturbed by the barking. Rosemary McCormick initiated a warrant for Athalia's arrest on April 23, 1973, which was also three days before Mrs. Fetter died. Patti Stanford stayed out of it at that point, preferring to write a long letter full of grievances against Athalia to Judge Charles Mathis and note, "I feel like I'm in the middle of a nightmare." Neither woman mentioned the death of her next-door neighbor or offered condolences to Athalia.

As the dispute escalated, Athalia sought to discredit Colonel McCormick and Alan Stanford but not their wives, Rosemary and Patti. This is curious. After all, the women were home more than the men, and the complaint about the barking dogs originated with them. Clearly, the origin of Athalia's vendetta against the McCormicks and against Alan Stanford, in particular, has more behind it, although the history, at this point, is lost.

It is also likely that Athalia was unwell. She was her mother's sole caretaker for years, a strenuous and a heartbreaking task. Her sister, Geraldine, mentioned several times in her deposition that Athalia was "run-down." Many of her friends and acquaintances remarked at how thin she was, and in pictures, she looked gaunt. Frances Bemis remarked that Athalia seemed "distraught and nervous, but I was told that she was always like that."

On the day of her death, James mentioned that Athalia "had to go to the bathroom" on the ride home from Jacksonville. Indeed, she was in such a hurry to make it to the bathroom that when she arrived home, she left her keys in the back door and put the groceries on the floor. After Athalia's death, Geraldine found "a bloody mass" and a tampon in a paper bag in the bathroom trash. At fifty-six, Athalia had surely been through menopause, and her sister, Geraldine, confirmed this in her deposition. If Athalia was experiencing postmenopausal "break-through bleeding," she may very well have been quite ill. Gynecologists consider such symptoms serious and as possible evidence of uterine or cervical cancer.

Athalia endured many life-changing events in a matter of two years. She made a major move to another city. Her mother died. She had gotten married. And it was likely she was ill. Any one of those experiences creates a tremendous amount of stress. One can surmise that Athalia, liberated from her mother's bedside for the first time in years and emboldened by her marriage to James Lindsley, was finally free to express her frustration with her neighbors. Going after Patti and Rosemary was not enough to appease her. She wanted to hit them all where it hurt.

But she was the one who got hurt. Ironically, on the day that Athalia was brutally murdered, there was not a peep from the dogs locked in the garage. None of the detectives even noticed they were there. Zsa Zsa, Margherita's old and beloved pet, walked through the house looking for Athalia.

The St. Augustine humane society picked them all up the next day.

WHAT ATHALIA KNEW

I'm not going to quit until I run him out of town.
—Athalia Ponsell Lindsley

In Spanish, the meaning of the name Athalia is "guard tower." In Hebrew, its meaning is "God is great." Supposedly, people with this name have a deep inner desire to create and to express themselves, often in public speaking, acting, writing or singing. They yearn to have beauty around them in their homes and in their work environments. Their analysis of people and world events may make them seem aloof and sometimes even melancholy.

She was born Athalia Anne Fetter. Her birthplace is listed as Toledo, Ohio, but if that is true, her mother, Margherita, flew from their home in Cuba to give birth in the States. Perhaps she wished to avoid future citizenship issues for young Athalia. America never relinquished Guantanamo to the Cubans, but it did surrender the satellite island that the Fetters called home in the early part of the twentieth century.

The Isle of Pines, known today as the Isla de la Juventud (Isle of Youth), is an island off Cuba previously owned by America and controlled by wealthy Americans. Columbus presumably landed there in the fifteenth century. In the early twentieth century, anyone could go there by catching a flight from Miami.

That is what the young Ohioan Margherita Gardner did on a vacation where she met Charles Franklin Fetter. She was an intelligent and adventurous woman, well educated, with an interest in writing. Charles was from Kansas, trained as a pharmacist, and he was ten years older than she was. He was also a pioneer, a colonist and "the owner of a chain of stores he established in 1905." He "pulled the switch" on December 25, 1916, giving the Isle of Pines "its first electric lights." He financed a telephone line on the island. Margherita married him on July 5, 1916. Athalia was born approximately thirteen months later.

Athalia lived near the Caribbean Sea on the balmy island known for its forests of pine trees until she was nine years old. Her sister, Geraldine, two years younger, was born during that time as well. It must have been an idyllic environment, tropical, with the sound of the surf crashing near the cape. But it was not long term.

The Fetters, and other Americans, lived in Cuba by virtue of the Platt Amendment, introduced to Congress in 1901. The Platt Amendment controlled Cuban foreign policy, and it declared that the Isle of Pines was not part of Cuba but rather part of America just like Guantanamo Bay. Cuba could not claim either territory unless the United States agreed.

The Cubans hated the amendment, and they wanted the Isle of Pines back. Sensing trouble, as early as 1924, Margherita and her friend Harriet Wheeler began lobbying Washington, D.C., to keep the Isle of Pines as part of the United States and to ignore a growing national fervor among the Cubans to take the island back.

By 1926, things had taken a turn for the worse for the Fetter family. In spite of his altruistic and friendly relations with native Cubans, anti-American sentiment had taken root. Charles was convicted of "sedition" and then pardoned and released. Shortly thereafter, the Fetter family relocated to the Riverside mansion in Jacksonville, Florida. By 1936, President Roosevelt had ratified the Platt Amendment as part of a conciliatory "good neighbor" policy. Cuba hoisted its own flag over the Isle of Pines, ensuring that Americans could not return there to live.

The Fetter family did not return to their island in the Caribbean. Athalia and Geraldine graduated from high school in Jacksonville, Florida. Athalia married a man named Dick Hyman when she was only eighteen. The marriage lasted two years. By the time their father, Charles, died in 1937 "after an illness of several weeks," Athalia and Geraldine were living in New York City.

In New York City, Athalia and her sister lived together in an apartment surrounded by people of every nationality and background. Both young women listed their occupations as "modeling and advertising." It was around this time that Athalia and Geraldine adopted the surname "Ponselle," presumably as a stage name. Athalia, in particular, showed great promise for success and fame in the big city.

As a Powers model, she was featured in numerous ads. She was a "Chevy girl," and she promoted Listerine toothpaste. She was in a 1945 ad in *Life* magazine for Kreml shampoo: "Miss Athalia Ponselle another divinely beautiful Powers girl who has discovered the remarkable beautifying action of Kreml shampoo. Teen age girls glamour bathe your hair like gorgeous Powers models."

Athalia sang in the ensemble as the Senorita in the musical comedy *Viva O'Brien*, which ran on Broadway at the Majestic Theatre for a few weeks in 1941. She was a regular on the TV game show *Winner Takes All*. Puff pieces planted in newspapers by agents described Athalia as the "face and figure gal."

Tall, blond and willowy, with high cheekbones and a slender figure, Athalia had a love life that made the gossip columns. She dated Joseph Kennedy Jr., and an engagement was rumored. After he died, she dated many men, and some of her liaisons made it into the papers. In 1942, Walter Winchell mentioned that "the Lieutenant F. Baeler-Athalia Ponsell [by then she'd dropped the *e* on her surname] wedding set for yesterday is off for good." In 1945, gossip columnist Dorothy Kilgallen linked Athalia to the famous stage manager of the Sea Island Club Ken MacSarin, an eccentric who subsisted solely on an egg diet.

In those days, a woman's career as a model waned when she hit the age of thirty. By 1947, Athalia was back in Jacksonville, living in the Riverside mansion. Somewhere, in the ensuing years, she married an insurance and real estate agent, Charles H. Blume. She had stepsons, but after she was divorced in 1962, there was no record of any consequent contact with the Blume family. By then, Geraldine had married, started a family and was living in Hawaii, running an art gallery. Margherita's health was failing, and Athalia served as caretaker. When she worked, she sold real estate, but somewhere along the line, her license lapsed. She took courses at college, but she never got a degree.

However, she was far from idle. In Jacksonville, Athalia dabbled in politics, ran for public office and took up some of her mother's club memberships, which included League of American Pen Women, Daughters of the American Revolution, Descendants of the Knights of the Garter, Magna Carter Dames and Americans of Royal Descent. As Athalia liked guns, she owned several and was "quite a wonderful shot," attending target practice with the Jacksonville police. She wrote a book about gardening and patented a household device.

Athalia and the "Pen Women" in her home on Marine Street. *Courtesy of Philip Whitley and the* St. Augustine Record.

And so the years passed, pleasantly, perhaps uneventfully. Athalia, a vibrant woman, passionate about causes and keenly intelligent, may have been bored. The neighborhood around Riverside was changing. So she decided to move to a place where she had pleasant school girl memories, settling on the white Spanish-style mansion on Marine Street with the big yard and the sunny rooms. Unfortunately, it was a fateful transition where she found herself embroiled in a verifiable feud.

After the McCormicks and the Stanfords ensured that she was fined for disturbing the peace and she got rid of most of her dogs, Athalia hired J.E. Manning, a tree surgeon, to cut back a pecan tree and a Canford tree to the property line between her house and the Stanfords' house. This action incensed the Stanfords. Then, according to Patti Stanford, Athalia planted "10 foot high" bamboo across the city easement at the corner of the Stanford driveway. Patti got the city to remove it as "a visual obstruction."

Thwarted again, Athalia wrote a letter to the commanding officer of the National Guard in reference to Colonel McCormick. The letter has not survived, so no one knows what she said. However, it is safe to presume that it was not complimentary information. Nothing came of the letter, and Athalia abandoned the colonel and turned to Alan Stanford. And Alan Stanford was much more vulnerable to her retaliatory efforts.

Athalia showed up at the news office of the *St. Augustine Record* to do some research on him. Anne Heymen, now a retired reporter, recalled that Athalia was tall, gorgeous and "intimidating." According to Managing Editor Patrick Lynn, Athalia "requested that a staff member be assigned to help her dig up information on Alan Stanford." In Lynn's words, when he "politely declined," Athalia "walked out of the office in a huff."

She must have been back, however, because she was a thorough woman. She found plenty of information. She fueled rumors that Alan was receiving county materials at his home for his own projects. Ironically, Assistant State Attorney Richard Watson, who was part of the prosecuting team at Athalia's murder trial, cleared Alan of this charge, claiming that it came from a "disgruntled employee." There were plenty of disgruntled employees.

Documented in St. Johns County city commission minutes in 1972 and 1973 are scores of road and bridge employees who came and went. Stanford tried to fire his interim predecessor, Peter Hardeman. Stanford fired Eddie Lightsey's son, and Lightsey was a highly ranked St. Johns County deputy. Stanford fired Clyde Woolever, an employee who showed up to criticize the paving job on Joe Ashton Road. Heads rolled at every commission meeting.

Then Commissioner Green ordered an investigation into "certain purchases made by Stanford" and the high employee turnover (155 percent), which was highlighted at a December 11 meeting in 1973 when a "delegation from the Road and Bridge Department" showed up to complain about working seven days a week without overtime pay. Stanford was not interested in their grievances. He asked the men if they had "permission from their supervisor" to attend a county meeting, as though public meetings weren't open to, well, the public.

Athalia showed up often at commission meetings, blatantly and publicly challenging Stanford's competence, complaining about his high salary and criticizing him for signing documents as the county engineer when he lacked the credentials to do so. A condition of Alan's employment required him to take the test to qualify as a professional engineer. He failed the test once in March 1973, and if he took it again, it is not mentioned in the ensuing commission minutes.

Whatever her reasons, it is unfair to paint Athalia solely as a vigilante for going after Stanford. James Lindsley formally introduced Athalia to the city commissioners as his wife and echoed her concerns about the condition of St. Johns County roads. At least one letter to the editor in the *St. Augustine Record* was titled "Hooray for Mrs. Lindsley," and there were plenty of complaints about Stanford's job performance as documented by local citizens. Another letter complaining about the drainage of Roscoe Boulevard and the appropriation for the road being used elsewhere was titled, "Watergate in St. Johns County." But such criticisms are not unusual for anyone in a public position. What is unusual is how Stanford fought back. In public, he was composed and polite. Privately, he was vengeful.

Shortly after her mother died, Athalia entertained a group of friends from Jacksonville. As they were leaving, she stood in the front of her house waving them off. Alan Stanford pulled up in his county car and motioned Athalia over. "You're a vicious evil woman," he said, "and one day I'm going to fix you."

Athalia did not take Stanford's threat lightly. She told James about it and also their mutual friend, a contractor named Gavin Laurie Jr. When Geraldine came to visit, she told her, "That man over there, that Alan Stanford, is going to kill me." James said afterward that Athalia repeated Stanford's threat at a public commission meeting, but there is no record of it in the official minutes. The threat is documented in a private addendum to the minutes provided by Ira Inman, a deputy clerk to Sheriff Garrett, in early February 1974.

The meeting in October 1973 was a particularly contentious one. First, James Lindsley complained that he and some friends drove out to Joe Ashton Road and encountered a sign that read, "Drive at your own risk, road under water." Alan said the sign was just meant to slow down traffic. Then Athalia addressed the commission members. "You are pouring taxpayer money down a rathole," she complained, referring to Alan Stanford's $20,000 salary and his lack of credentials. Athalia asked the commissioners why Alan got a raise higher than the 11 percent everyone else got.

Herbie Wiles, Stanford's loyal friend and the board chairman, said, "We feel like, I personally, Mrs. Lindsley, feel like he's worth it." Wiles denied that it was necessary for a civil engineer to do Stanford's job, even though obtaining that credential had been a condition of his employment.

Athalia said, "You just stated a while ago everybody got an 11% increase on their little ole salary so how come he gets more? Now, you as an individual, because you believe he should have more, then you want to dish it out. Well, how come you can justify that?" What Athalia said was true. Not one employee in the county was making within $12,000 of Alan's salary, even if he'd been there fifteen, twenty, twenty-five years. And Alan had only served for two years.

Herbie said, "Well, Mrs. Lindsley, I feel that I am elected by the people and trying to represent them the best way possible and in this particular—"

Athalia cut him off: "You're only one. They're others."

Herbie Wiles said, "I want to remind you that I am aware that you are a neighbor of the Stanfords and that y'all have had neighbor problems and I feel you are bringing yourself—"

Athalia was speaking at the same time. She said, "I sure am. That's true. My life has been threatened too, I'll tell you. You mention personal things, he threatened my life."

Alan was recognized by Commissioner Green. He said, "I'd like to state, Mr. Chairman, that that's a lie, that is not true. Everyone began speaking at once. This was not uncommon at commission meetings that Athalia attended. Even routine agendas were rarely dull. Athalia also complained publicly at a commission meeting that Alan put sugar in the gas tank of her Cadillac while she was out of town with James attending a wedding. James Lindsley was also suspicious of Alan, and he confronted him about the incident at the Stanford home. James had a reputation for a temper and for swinging with his fists first and asking questions later. Stanford denied it, but he was conveniently working on his roof at that moment and was out of James's reach.

It probably seemed to Athalia that Alan was going to get away with what she perceived as his dishonesty, his slyness and his cowardly chicanery. Then her vendetta began to bear some fruit. She had taken matters into her own hands and finally landed Alan Stanford in the hot water she felt he deserved.

On a Wednesday afternoon, at 4:15 p.m. (documented time), January 23, 1974, the day of Athalia's murder, Stanford received two visitors in his county office from the Florida Department of Professional and Occupational Regulations. Thomas J. Murphy Jr. and Elmer Emrich were investigators for the Florida State Board. They were there at Athalia's request.

Athalia handwrote a letter to the executive director on December 4, 1973, using the royal pronoun *we* to convey solidarity among St. Augustine citizens:

> *We feel it our duty to inform of the apparent malpractice of a man who appears to be passing himself off as a certified engineer. He signs county legal documents as the County Engineer, when as far as we can ascertain he has no engineering degree in any field.*
>
> *This seeming chicanery casts a shadow on the Professional Engineering Society of the State of Florida, comparable to a "Quack" practicing medicine.*
>
> *By bringing this to your attention, we hope it can be investigated and rectified.*

The executive director, J.Y. Read, wrote back confirming that Stanford was planning to retake the engineering examination in April. In mid-January,

Athalia's lawyer, George Stallings, wrote to Elmer Emrich informing him of Alan's lack of credentials. But Emrich had already heard from the executive director, and he wrote Athalia that "the content of your communication has been carefully reviewed, and you may be assured that this Board will afford this matter appropriate review."

The "review" included an investigation to determine whether Alan violated Florida statutes or the Rules of Professional Conduct. Although Stanford later testified that "the matter was cleared up" during the meeting, that was not the case. In a February 1 interview with Special Agent Dallas Herring, Murphy conceded that he mentioned to Stanford that "he was in possible violation of two Florida State Statutes, 471 and 472."

Afterward, Murphy and Emrich both confirmed to Special Agent Dallas Herring that Stanford was cool and collected during the January 23 meeting in his office. Mr. Emrich stated that Stanford acted as anyone would have expected and did not show any more than normal concern about the situation. He added, "Mr. Stanford did not give any indication that would lead me to believe that he [Stanford] would go out and kill Mrs. Lindsley."

Stanford spent some time explaining to Emrich and Murphy the problems that Mrs. Lindsley caused in the neighborhood after the court ordered her to get rid of her dogs. She was trying to get him fired, Stanford averred, as if that explained everything. Yet Murphy added to Herring that "[i]f I [Murphy] had been approached in a similar situation, I would have been upset and quite angered by such an interview, and I felt that Stanford was 'too cool' for the situation."

Patti Stanford had already complained to Judge Mathis that Athalia "endangered her husband's employment" with her public ridicule and harassment. Now it seemed that Athalia had a foothold in finally realizing her stated goal of "running him [Stanford] out of town."

The meeting lasted about an hour, and the pair left at 5:15 p.m. Emrich and Murphy took a drive down Marine Street around 5:30 p.m. (documented time) on January 23 to verify the location of Athalia's home. They planned to call on her the following day and interview her. Both men reported that the street was quiet and there was no one in view. They went back to their motel room in the Holiday Inn near Interstate 95 and State Road 16. There, they passed a quiet evening.

The state investigators mentioned the letters they received from Athalia, but they did not allow Alan to see them. Of course, their interview with Athalia, which they may have mentioned to Stanford, never occurred. The "next day" was too late.

Athalia was a Leo, and her horoscope for January 23 read, "You may not be able to accomplish ALL that you schedule but with an optimistic attitude and sincere endeavor you can, nevertheless, give a distinguished performance." Or, as her widower, James, said afterward, "She simply had more courage than discretion."

WHAT ALAN KNEW

I'm going to send her back where she came from.
—Alan Griffith Stanford Jr.

Athalia Ponsell Lindsley and Alan Stanford had nothing in common, and that included their upbringing. Athalia was born on a balmy island in the Caribbean, and Alan was born to a big house in the suburbs of Atlanta. Athalia had a working and a well-educated mother who questioned authority, to the point of lobbying the U.S. government in Washington, D.C. Alan's mother was a housewife. Athalia and her family were adventurous, living and traveling to many points in the world. Alan lived in the same house from the age of five until he went off to college.

Athalia followed her own interests in modeling, marketing and research, and although influenced by Margherita's independence and sense of adventure, she did not become an academic and an educator like her mother. Instead, she forged her own path in New York City as a minor celebrity who knew how to market her looks and her talent. Alan was named after his father and, for a year, went to Clemson, his father's alma mater. He followed the same career path as his father to become a civil engineer. Only Alan Jr. never quite made it.

Certainly, that was a disappointment, as civil engineering was his original major, according to his first draft card. His eventual lack of that coveted degree, which Athalia harped on, could have easily led to his dismissal as county manager. No one knows to what extent Alan's inability to live up to his father's accomplishments debilitated him or if he exhibited signs of mental illness before January 23, 1974.

Where Athalia was described as a hothead and a rabble-rouser, newspaper articles and private testimony repeatedly depicted Alan as "quiet," "soft-spoken," "calm" and "cool." But other accounts of an out-of-control temper are recalled as well. There is a story that he flew into a rage and destroyed the sensor on a compressor at the county office after tiring of his clerks bickering about the office temperature. Certainly, Patti Stanford's later testimony in her deposition can only be described as incoherent and fearful. Alan himself testified, "The trouble over the dogs affected her [Patti's] nervous system." Perhaps she had other reasons for her bad nerves.

Yet on the surface, Alan led the charmed life of the privileged white southern male. The house he grew up in stands today on a big lot in a nice Fulton County suburb. Built in 1930, it has three bedrooms, two and a half baths, a fireplace, a finished basement and almost three thousand square feet of living space.

Alan was named after his father. His sister, Lydia, two years older, was named after her mother. Alan Sr. grew up in South Carolina and graduated from Clemson with a degree in civil engineering. Lydia was a stay-at-home mom and a Yankee from New York who was two years older than her husband.

Alan's sister, Lydia, didn't go to college, but straight out of high school, Alan Jr. dutifully attended one year of Clemson, which at the time was an all-white, all-male military college in South Carolina and the alma mater of its senator, segregationist Strom Thurmond. When America entered World War II, Alan transferred to the United States Merchant Marine Academy in Kings Port, New York. He held a "B" average, joined the reserves and, according to his résumé, received a degree in marine engineering. He obtained another bachelor's degree in business administration, marketing and finance from Emory University in Atlanta.

By 1948, Alan was living in Atlanta and married to Patricia Angela Mullen. They were the perfect young American couple of the mid-twentieth century: white, middle class, southern and traditional. A former frat boy (Phi Delta Theta), Alan belonged to the Kiwanis, and he was a vestryman at the Episcopal church they both attended. Patti was a Georgia girl, twenty-one years old, a pretty brunette and willing to travel where her husband needed to go to obtain work.

Alan's first professional job was in Atlanta as a Southern Mills sales representative for industrial textiles. In 1956, the young couple moved to Dallas, Texas, where Alan worked as a general sales manager for Ling-

Temco-Vought (LTV), selling industrial and commercial component parts in the aerospace industry. By then, the pair had two daughters, Sherry and Patricia. In 1963, the couple moved to Hagerstown, Maryland, where Alan held yet another account and management position for Fairchild Hiller Corporation. Within the next five years, he changed jobs three times—twice with Fairchild Hiller—and worked within the realm of marketing and management for heavy equipment companies.

Eventually, the Maryland manufacturing company transferred Alan to St. Augustine, where he sold aircraft parts. By then, his youngest daughter, Annette, had been born. In 1971, he caught wind of the county manager position for St. Johns—probably from his friend Commissioner Herbie Wiles—and he formally applied for it in December. Since the job required a civil engineering degree, Alan listed "engineering functions included during the past 16 years of experience" on his résumé. These included "research and development," "construction equipment design and fabrication" and "aircraft equipment invention."

Of the six applicants, Alan was unanimously chosen for the job by the county commissioners with the understanding that he obtain his civil engineering certification sooner rather than later. They promised him a raise when he got it, although his starting salary of $17,500 was good by 1972 standards. He was on the job by January 17. By then he was already on Athalia's radar.

Alan later testified that Athalia's public attacks on his competence and on his lack of credentials were taken "in a light vein" and that he and fellow commissioners just thought she was "nutty." He described having virtually no communication with her and said he was "not particularly" bothered by living next door to someone who hated him.

Documented facts show a different story. Nancy Powell—longtime St. Augustine resident, Athalia's friend and consequent coauthor of *Bloody Sunset*—later testified during his trial that a week before the murder, Alan called her up in 1973 asking if she had any "dirt" on Athalia and how many times Athalia was married. Nancy was the managing bureau editor for the *Florida Times-Union*, but whatever she knew about her friend, she kept to herself. Then Alan told her that if Athalia didn't lay off the public attacks, he would "send her back where she came from."

Sheriff Garrett testified during his deposition that he received a call from Alan around this time asking him to check into Athalia's background. The sheriff said, "Well, I told him I couldn't, I dealt mostly in hard crime cases; I didn't have time to go into a thorough background on things like that. I said I would check the files of Duval County and that's about all I did."

The January 22 commission meeting was the last of a series of humiliating debacles for Alan Stanford at the hands of Athalia Ponsell Lindsley. Athalia had been busy interviewing Stanford's fired employees, who were, naturally, critical of Stanford, as were several other St. Augustine residents. They were critical of Stanford's treatment of county roads, which often flooded and were pocked with potholes. They were critical of an "experimental project on Cabbage Road that was falling apart after only two months." It was falling apart because the road was only an inch thick, and trucks hauled garbage into the neighborhood and dumped it to enrich the soil for pine trees, a "project" devised by the commissioners. Residents said the smell was "nauseating," and there were flies everywhere. They'd already notified the Department of Pollution Control, which described the commissioners' "solid waste pilot project" as a "landfill." Herbie Wiles explained, "It was a means of handling the mounting garbage problem."

A delegation of these citizens living next to "the project" and a county employee, Clyde Woolever, appeared with Athalia at the Tuesday, January 22 meeting. Athalia said the road at Cabbage Hammock was "deplorable," and Joe Ashton was "ripply." Athalia asked Alan what degree he held and what his experience in building roads was. Clyde Woolever complained about the disintegrating paving job Alan authorized on Joe Ashton Road. He said the road was only an inch thick instead of the six- to eight-inch standard used by engineers. Alan Stanford countered that the road was four inches thick, although at a commission meeting in November 1973, he "advised" that only two inches of compacted asphalt be used for that particular job. Apparently, Athalia's concerns about Alan's engineering credentials were founded in more than malice.

Woolever was fired from his county job the next day, January 23, for "shabby" work. Alan contended at a February 12 commission meeting that Woolever's "attendance at the January 22nd meeting had nothing to do with it [termination of employment]." After signing the papers terminating Clyde Woolever's employment on the afternoon of January 23, Alan learned from two representatives of the Florida board that he was violating the law by misrepresenting his public position. Clearly, eliminating Woolever was not enough. His job was in jeopardy because of Athalia Ponsell Lindsley.

Alan's mother and his wife were homemakers. He was a southern man and unaccustomed to women such as Athalia. Alan was not stupid, but it is clear that he was no mental giant either. In terms of ingenuity and intellect,

Athalia far surpassed him. She openly collected evidence to dispose of him and aired it in a public forum. He poured sugar into the gas tank of her car when she was out of town, called around to find damaging gossip and privately threatened her.

The pressures of his job were enormous. Bad news was coming at him from every side. Although his friend Herbie Wiles still defended him, the rest of the commissioners were getting tired of the ruckus Athalia caused at commission meetings. And now he was being investigated by the Florida Board of Engineers for breaking the law.

On his drive home from the office, Alan must have been literally steaming. He owned a big expensive house on the nicest street in St. Augustine. He was the sole support of his wife and two of his daughters. What would he do if he were turned away from his job in disgrace? Emrich and Murphy planned an interview with Athalia the following day. Was there any way he could stop the interview from occurring?

Alan parked near Charlotte Street at the rear of the house. There is no doubt that he was in an agitated frame of mind as he approached his home. He headed right for the kitchen sink and quickly, by his own admission, downed two drinks. He opened up the newspaper. Athalia pulled up in her driveway.

What happened next is hard to decipher. In fiction, there is such a thing as "an unreliable narrator." The term refers to a character whose credibility is seriously compromised. If the murder of Athalia Ponsell Lindsley were a fictional drama instead of nonfiction, and Alan, Patti and Patricia Stanford were telling her story, they would be the unreliable narrators.

In real life, it was factually clear that in relaying the events that resulted in the near decapitation of their neighbor on January 23, the Stanfords were all figuratively lying their own heads off.

THE TIMELINE

Time keeps on slipping, slipping, slipping…
      —"Fly Like an Eagle," Steve Miller Band

I wish I hadn't looked.
      —Patti Stanford

It was more than the blood trail leading from Athalia's front steps to the concrete wall of Alan's property and then to the point where his county car was parked and no further. It was more than Locke McCormick's initial eyewitness account of the murder, the feud between the neighbors, the blood-soaked evidence later obtained from the Sebastian River and the consequent recovery of the rusted murder weapon. The most damning evidence against Alan Stanford was his own testimony and the testimony of his wife and his daughter about the events of January 23.

One could argue the facts of the case backward and forward, but there is no disputing the inherent weakness of their documented testimonies. Their recalls were riddled with inconsistencies, contradictions, backtracking and startling lapses of memory from start to finish. A February 1, 1975 newspaper article in the *Florida Times-Union* headlined, "Element of Time Puzzling in Trial" captured only a fraction of the obtrusive wall of meaningless words that accompanied the deposition and testimony of Alan Stanford and of his immediate family. However, within the morass of their recount of events, a few nuggets of truth were unwittingly revealed.

"It was horrible," Patti Stanford said at her husband's trial. "I wish I hadn't looked. I never saw so much blood." According to Patti, she witnessed the aftermath of the crime scene from the fenced-in perimeter of the front lawn when she ran out in response to Rosemary McCormick's cry. According to Patti, she took a brief look and ran back inside. One could argue that there was not enough time, and she was not close enough, to register an impression such as the one she gave.

But if she saw it happen and then encountered her husband afterward in the backyard, her story makes sense. Patti admitted that she could look out her window from her kitchen sink and see into her neighbor's front yard. As Athalia's assailant swung the machete, he hit her nine times, mostly in the upper body and in the neck. There are two carotid arteries, one on each side of the neck. Each of these divides into two, giving an interior and an exterior artery. A cut, such as one delivered from a machete, would slice the artery faster than a stab wound. Death comes once blood loss is so great that blood pressure drops drastically, and in Athalia's case, that probably happened within less than a minute. But cutting a carotid artery makes a lot of mess. Blood literally comes out like a fountain. It goes up the walls of a room. It went up the left exterior wall of Athalia's home. It would make quite an impression on someone watching.

In the aftermath, Alan Stanford's most fervent supporters clung to the belief that Patti Stanford would not have stayed with her husband if she knew he was guilty. Alan's lawyer said, "The state's contention that Mrs. Stanford witnessed her husband coming across the fence with the bloody clothes and machete is ridiculous. It's absurd to believe that Mrs. Stanford and her daughter would still be living with Stanford if they witnessed him coming from the crime scene."

Clearly, witnessing a spouse wielding a bloody machete would make any wife run in the opposite direction. But were there were other factors at play?

Dominic Nicklo, one of the first officers on the scene, was convinced that Patti, and perhaps Patricia as well, saw Alan Stanford attack Athalia. Their testimony and their actions would seem to confirm rather than to refute that theory. Officer O'Loughlin held the same opinion and even remarked that Alan seemed about to confess at one point in the consequent interrogation when they were interrupted by the arrival of Sheriff Garrett. Sheriff Garrett said that Alan Stanford kept walking up and down his own front lawn the night of the murder. Was he trying to overhear what the officers were saying?

There are many unknowns, unknowns that can never be answered, but enough time has passed in order to view the events and the amassed evidence of January 23 objectively. In order to cut through the Stanfords' unintelligible and garbled testimony, it is necessary to try to fit together what they said happened with contradictory testimony and with common sense.

Patti Stanford and Patricia Stanford were each interviewed four times: the day of the murder, the following day, at a formal deposition and at Alan's murder trial. The testimony of Patricia's friend Hunter Barnett and Hunter's stepfather, Jesse Miller, provided further information as to an accurate timeline of the gruesome events that followed.

Let's start with Patti Stanford. Officer Larrow first interviewed Patti at an undetermined time on January 23, the night of the murder. She said she was serving supper when she heard the screams and ran out the front door. But by the very next morning, when she talked to Detective Nicklo, her story had changed. Here are some crucial excerpts from her taped interview to use for comparison with her own, her daughter's and her husband's consequent testimonies:

> *Patti: We finished supper. I heard screams…an awful scream. The minute I heard it, I told Patricia to take the baby upstairs to watch television and I went flying out the door.*
> *Nicklo: Which door did you go out?*
> *Patti:* Hesitation. *It must have been the front door.* Hesitates. *Oh, I can't remember which door I went out…I was in a total state of confusion.*
> *Nicklo: Did you see anybody in the area at all…*
> *Patti: No, but then I would not have paid attention—the car traffic, it's what we live by all the time. See, out front.*
> *Nicklo: Were you home most of the day?*
> *Patti: I was home all day until I took Patricia to her tennis game. That was at—*hesitation*—it must have been around 4 p.m.*
> *Nicklo: What time did you get back?*
> *Patti: I got back around 5:30.*
> *Nicklo: Did you notice anybody in the neighborhood who was strange to the neighborhood…*
> *Patti: No—See, we live in a funny neighborhood—always people walking up and down Marine Street. It's not like a residential street, that if you see somebody strange and say "there is a stranger" because those streets evidently going down to the hospital and back…*
> *Nicklo: What time did your husband get home?*
> *Patti: He was here. I said, "Hurry, let's eat…" then we ate and he said, "I've got to go to the office and get a slide rule and his book."*

Nicklo: What time did you get home from the tennis courts?
Patti: It was either 5:00 or 5:15 or 5:30—
Nicklo: How long after you got home did your husband leave?
Hesitation
Patti: I guess it was after we ate supper. So—I wonder what I was doing.
Nicklo: You did eat supper, right?
Patti: Yes.
Nicklo: You came home around 5:15, you fixed supper, and your husband was there, and he hung around until you got through working and you all sat down and ate supper. Right?
Patti: Right.
Nicklo: And then he went to the office—roughly what time would you say that was?
Patti: Gosh—that's hard to say—because if I was cooking at 5:30. I'll tell you what creates my house so chaotic is because of the three and a half year old and 18 year old is always tearing here or there, so times with me are yet as I say—
Nicklo: The time factor is very important.
Patti: I can't give it to you exactly, because we had been eating supper, he went out to the office—I don't remember exactly what I did then—
Nicklo: Let's go through the sequence again—

Patti said that she left at 4:00 p.m., picked up Patricia's friend Hunter Barnett and took them to the tennis courts while she went shopping at Winn-Dixie. Then she took Hunter home and got back to Marine Street between 5:15 p.m. and 5:30 p.m. Her husband was home. Nicklo asked how long it took to cook dinner. Patti didn't know.

Patti: Isn't that ridiculous—it's so stupid not to know how long it took you to finish supper.
Nicklo: 20 minutes?
Patti: I had steak, I fixed a salad, because that's funny, before I had this baby, I could have told you exactly how long I did everything—literally, but know, but now that I had a toddler around, I am not so indoctrinated anymore.
Nicklo: 30 to 45 minutes?
Patti: Yes, I guess it would.
Nicklo: …somewhere around six?
Patti: Yes.

Nicklo: What time did your husband come home?

Patti: He was home when I got here.

Nicklo: Did your husband have anything to drink last night?

Patti: I think he did.

Nicklo: Where did he generally fix his drinks?

Patti: Right there at the sink.

Nicklo: Did your husband change clothes yesterday? What was he wearing when you came home?

Patti: I have no idea.

Nicklo: No idea?

Patti: No, I'll tell you why, because normally he comes home, he changes clothes, and he goes out to work on building the garage, and we got the plumbing thing upstairs—so like I say I just tore into the house…I really just gave him a quick kiss and didn't even look at his clothes, but I assume he had his work clothes on. Only because every night he has them.

Nicklo: What time does your husband generally come home.

Patti: It just depends, it could be 5:00, 5:30, 6:00 or 7:00, there is no pattern.

Nicklo: Do you remember what he wore to work yesterday?

Patti: No! I apologize, but as I said our race is so fast and we go through the same thing every morning…

Nicklo: From the time you first heard the screaming, how much time elapsed between your husband having left for work?

Patti: Gosh, I think the trouble being that when I went running down the—

Hesitation

Nicklo: What time did you get through with the dishes.

Patti: I cleaned up the dishes, talked to Pat. [hesitation] I don't believe I have any idea. What makes it hard when your mind is running two different people, no, I don't guess you don't know. It makes it a little harder on me as I say because the baby she is a full time thing, but here again I was trying desperately to find her shoes for my 18 year old…what a queer thing to lose—I guess I was going about my normal fast hurry thing around here.

Nicklo: Did you get up from the dinner table and go straight out there?

Patti: Yeah. [Nicklo asked again if Patti could remember what her husband was wearing.]…*He puts on his work clothes, I mean that's just a normal—with the two giant projects we've had for months now, that's the normal—so I don't pay any attention on unless he goes to the vestry meeting, but last night wasn't a meeting night.* [Nicklo asked whether Alan puts on his work clothes right away.]...*Yes, as soon as he gets in.*

Nicklo: Let's run through this time sequence one more time...because... you may have seen something unconsciously or your husband may have seen something.

Patti: I don't even remember...I become so busy...once I start running fast...bought four bags of groceries—at Winn Dixie—brought in the groceries and started supper—it would have to be about 5:30.

Nicklo: Then you cooked supper.

Patti: Right—

Nicklo: What did you have?

Patti: Steak, green beans, black-eyed peas, lettuce and tomatoes.

Nicklo: Did your daughter help you?

Patti: No.

Nicklo: Then the family sat down and ate supper.

Patti: Right.

Nicklo: What time would you estimate you were through?

Patti: Gosh, I just don't have any way of estimating when I was through.

During this interview, the first in-depth one with Patti Stanford, Detective Nicklo keeps circling back to the improbable time frame that she presents.

Patti said that she left the house at 4:00 p.m. to pick up Patricia's friend, Hunter, and dropped both girls off at the tennis courts. Then she went grocery shopping, picked the girls up, dropped Hunter off and was home between 5:15 p.m. to 5:30 p.m. She and Patricia lugged four bags of groceries into the house and Patti unpacked and put them away by herself while her daughter went upstairs to try on a dress. Her husband was home. According to his employees, he wore a white dress shirt and dark trousers to the office every day. According to Emrich and Murphy, Alan wore a white dress shirt with button cuffs and dark trousers that day as well. But Patti, his wife, could not remember what he wore to work that morning. Still, she was pretty sure that he was in his cruddy "work around the house" clothes when she got home. Then she cooked supper, and she was pretty detailed about what they ate. (In Patti's subsequent deposition, she gave an account about how it took her three minutes to fry a steak.) She wanted Nicklo to believe that they all ate and then Alan got up and left to go back to work well before 6:00 p.m., the presumable time of Athalia's death.

Patti said in her first interview that she was serving dinner when she heard the screams. Then she said in her second interview that they were finished eating at the time of the screams. The third time, when she was interviewed on February 26 in the courthouse, Patti said that they were in the hall at the time. Later during the same interview, she said she was at the sink doing the dishes. Her account was so muddled, and it changed it so often, that it was clear that Patti was babbling. Twice she lost her temper with Nicklo. She hesitated at crucial points in this interview and in the subsequent interviews. She used the word *normal* more than five times over the course of all of the interviews and the words *tear* and *tore* and *fly* in improbable contexts. She used the word *indoctrinate*, as in denying that she was "so indoctrinated," perhaps subconsciously and desperately asserting to Nicklo that she had not been instructed, trained or coached in what to say. In an interview, she asked, "Who is it I keep telling this story to?" She was questioning jurisdiction, but "this story" implied something fabricated.

What was most notably absent was any empathy for Athalia, a neighbor she despised but who deserved human sympathy considering her brutal demise. Patti also did not display any real willingness to help, which again would be the automatic response of anyone whose neighbor was murdered— it was the response of the other neighbors interviewed by the police. Patti constructed a view of the neighborhood that depicted the sidewalks teeming with strangers, even though she went "flying" out her clearly unlocked door. Even after her neighbor was killed, Patti did not lock her doors or call anyone, Alan or the police, from the kitchen phone. She allowed Patricia to take Annette out to the backyard to the swing set and, later, allowed Patricia to drive herself to school for a meeting.

When her daughter Patricia and her daughter's friend Hunter were interviewed, things got even weirder. Although Patti had trouble remembering Hunter's name, calling her "that little girl," Hunter Barnett was honored on January 23 as "student of the month" by the St. Augustine Elks Lodge No. 829. Her picture was printed in the newspaper, and her accomplishments took up two and a half columns of print. She was a trustworthy and intelligent young woman, and more than a year later in court, Hunter asserted, under direct examination by Assistant State Attorney Richard Watson, that Patti and Patricia did not pick her up on January 23 for the tennis match until at least 4:20 p.m. She called them at the last minute saying that she needed a ride because her mother was out of town, and she looked at the clock when they arrived. According to Hunter, she and Patricia did not even begin to play tennis at Davenport Park until at least 4:25 p.m. She said that Mrs. Stanford drove off and didn't return for close to an hour. She and Patricia were finishing their tennis game when Patti arrived. Patti took Annette into the park and played with her near the swings. Then the teenagers "went and sort of ran around in the park with the little girl for a couple of minutes." Hunter asserted that she got home between 5:30 p.m. and 5:40 p.m. Her stepfather, Jessie Miller, was home at the time, and he confirmed Hunter's recollection, making the time she was dropped off nearer to 6:00 p.m.

The first time that Patricia Stanford was interviewed in depth occurred on February 1, 1974, at the St. Johns County Courthouse. Richard Watson, the assistant state attorney, courteously and gently questioned her. Patricia said she returned home from the tennis courts around 5:00 p.m. or 5:15 p.m. Then she amended the time to 5:30 p.m. She said her father wasn't home when she and her mother returned. She and her mother brought the groceries inside. She set the table, and her mother cooked dinner. A few minutes later, Alan turned up. She said only she, Annette and her mother sat down to eat around fifteen minutes later.

She said her father was standing by the sink, reading the paper and having a drink. He also played with Annette and changed into his "nasty old work clothes," although she could not remember what he was originally wearing. She said they were still eating when Alan left around 5:45 p.m. She and her mother said, "Goodbye" and "We'll see you later," which means that he changed his clothes, played with the baby, had a drink (he later admitted he had two drinks), looked at the paper and left abruptly for work to check on something he forgot (some dredging permits, which his secretary had already mailed), all within less than fifteen minutes. Watson asked Patricia if she heard her father's car start up, and she said she didn't.

She said she and her mother were still eating when she heard the screams. Her mother gave several different versions of what she was doing at the time. Regardless, every time the story is told, both women agreed that upon hearing the second set of screams, Patti said to her daughter, "You take the baby."

Patricia said, "See, the baby's little, you know, I feel as responsible for her as Mother does and so I just grabbed her and did whatever I could. So we stood at the back door and my neighbor, Mrs. McCormick, which is on the other side of the house, she was calling for Mother and Mother said, 'Well, what is it, what is it?' And she said, 'Patti, Patti, come here, quick.' So, finally, Mother said, 'You take the baby and do something with her,' and so Mother ran over there and she ran around the side of the house and then out the front and down there."

Watson asked, "Ran out of which door?"

Patricia said, "The back door. [Patti always contended she went out the front door.] She had already gone out the back door when she heard this second series of screams and she was standing there and you could see diagonally sort of into Mrs. McCormick's yard and she was standing there screaming for her, and she ran around the side of the house out front and down the street to Mrs. McCormick's house and she came back a little while later, I don't know how long it was, I said, you know, I asked her what happened and she said, 'Oh, it's terrible,' and she told me what she had seen."

Watson said, "Patty, I believe the window in your kitchen is rather high, you can't see out of that window sitting down?"

Patricia replied, "No, sir."

Watson established that there were two sets of screams, a few seconds apart, the first being Mrs. Lindsley's screams and the second being Mrs. McCormick's screams. Watson asked, "Now, your mother then got up when she heard Mrs. McCormick and went to the back door?"

Patricia said, "Yes, sir, she went outside the back door."

Watson asked, "When your mother came back in the house after she had been over there, did she say anything about your father, where is your father or anything?"

Patricia said, "No not then."

Watson asked, "She didn't ask where he was?"

Patricia said no. Watson asked her if she went to the back door when she heard the screams. Patricia told him she did: "Yes sir, Annette and I were standing at the back door and Mother was outside on the back patio."

Watson confirmed, "Your mother was in the back yard?" Patricia said her mother was standing on the back patio right outside the door. Watson asked her if she saw anybody come out of Mrs. Lindsley's yard.

Patricia said, "No, sir, because we just stood at the door and then I took the baby away." Patricia went upstairs with Annette and looked out her bedroom window. She saw Mrs. Lindsley lying dead in her own blood on the front steps next door. A little while later, she took Annette outside to swing on the swings in the backyard. Her mother was somewhere in the house, hysterical. No one called Alan at work. No one locked the doors. No one worried about Patricia and Annette alone in the yard less than a half hour after someone hacked her neighbor to death in broad daylight.

At some point—perhaps that night, perhaps a few days later—Patricia went over to talk to Locke McCormick. She asked him if he saw what happened. She may have been asking for her own information. She may have been asking to see how much he knew. She did tell her mother about his response, which was, "It could have been Mr. Lindsley, it could have been your daddy, it could have been my daddy." After initially identifying

Alan as the murderer ("Mr. Stanford is hitting Mrs. Ponsell"), Locke never specifically identified Alan again.

His words may have comforted Patricia if she never actually saw her father walk into the backyard covered in gore, as her mother almost certainly did after she sent the girls upstairs. But Colonel McCormick was on a hunting trip in Mexico. Jinx had an airtight account of his whereabouts. That left Alan.

Patricia didn't know about Jinx, but who knows how much she saw and who knows how much she knew? She said that her father walked into her bedroom the night of the twenty-third before she went to sleep "because he knew I was upset about it." Alan told her, "Don't worry. I had nothing to do with it."

But Patricia worried. She told Watson, "The woman [Mrs. Lindsley] caused him so much trouble I figured if they couldn't find him [the murderer] that they might point the finger at him."

Later, Patricia gave court testimony that the state attorney, Stephen Boyles, said "didn't add up." She said she was tired during the first interview and that she answered on "impulse." She said she and her mother definitely got home from the tennis courts at 5:15 p.m. During the trial, she said her father was there when they got home. She stated vehemently that after she and her mother had both seen Mrs. Lindsley's body, "There was no reason to lock the doors or stay inside. There are very few things that scare me." She insisted that there was no consequent discussion that night or ever with either her father or her mother about the murder that occurred next door. When asked if she wasn't curious, Patricia said, "Well, I had seen what happened out the window, but I didn't discuss it with anyone."

Was it a slip of the tongue? Alan Stanford was the most culpable suspect. His wife and his daughter surely knew it.

WHERE WAS ALAN?

Aquarius horoscope for January 23, 1974: "A day for astute thinking and equally wise follow-up. Try something different…"

—*Frances Drake*

B ased on evidence and testimony, the following is the most likely scenario for the events that occurred around dinnertime on Wednesday, January 23, 1974.

Although he claimed that he was home between 5:00 p.m. and 5:15 p.m. that night, and although his friend Commissioner Herbie Wiles said that he saw Alan on the road at 5:05 p.m., Alan Stanford's interview with Murphy and Emrich ended, by their account, at 5:15. p.m. Alan's office was empty when he left because both Jodi Hough, a technical clerk, and Hazel McCallum, his secretary, testified that he was still in a meeting when they left at 4:35 p.m.

It was rush hour, and from Lewis Speedway, it took Alan about twenty minutes to get home to Marine Street—maybe more. Officer Terrell G. Davis clocked the time on February 27, 1974, during a test drive from the county manager's office to Stanford's home. Not breaking the speed limit put him there at twenty-five minutes, thirty-five seconds. Going as quickly as possible took eighteen minutes, twenty seconds. That would place Alan at home between about 5:33 p.m. and 5:40 p.m., just around the time Athalia was seen leaving Jinx's office and about five or ten minutes before his wife and daughters got home, according to Hunter Barnett and Jessie Miller.

Alan said that when he got home, he first put on his old clothes in order to work on the garage. It is more likely that he headed straight to the kitchen sink and mixed himself a gin and tonic. He downed it quickly. By his own admission, he had two drinks. It could have been three. He said that he saw Athalia in her yard watering her plants, which was impossible because she was on her way home from 214 St. George Street. Why would she water plants and then be in such a hurry to get in the house that she'd leave the keys in the lock and the groceries on the floor?

Murphy and Emrich took a ride through the neighborhood around 5:30 p.m. to pinpoint Athalia's home, as they intended on speaking with her the following day. They saw no one home.

Alan's daughter Patricia said that he was reading the newspaper at some point in the kitchen on the late afternoon of January 23. In it, he saw an account of the humiliating commission meeting from the night before. There on the bottom of the front page of the *St. Augustine Record* was the headline, "Pine Tree Project, Road Draw Protests."

The article could have been worse. For one thing, a Stanford family friend, Jackie Feagin, wrote it. For another, Athalia's name was not even mentioned, and it portrayed the county commissioners in a worse light than it did Alan. There was even an excerpt about the county commissioners wanting to ban prohibitions against swimming pools in front yards. Still, it was an astonishing document highlighting gross incompetence on the part of the commissioners *and* the county manager. The contents made the palpable rage Athalia displayed at commission meetings almost understandable.

But not to Alan Stanford. "Garbage-enriched land" along Cabbage Hammock Road was one quote. "The road is not more than an inch thick" was another. "It's not the best road in the world," Wiles, the board chair, told the *Record.* Alan read the article, perhaps reliving the meeting, perhaps reliving every humiliating thing Athalia had said and done to him in the past year. She set Emrich and Murphy after him. She was going to get him fired. That looming threat seemed real to him at last.

According to Alan, he then abruptly left his house at 5:30 p.m. to go back to his office. This is preposterous based on documented evidence from a variety of sources. Athalia wouldn't even have been home by then. Alan probably wasn't even home yet. Most likely, his wife and daughter weren't either. In today's world, if he were really on the road after two or three strong drinks, he would be eligible for a DUI.

So, what really happened? The following scenario is supposition, but it is a logical reconstruction of the facts of that horrible day—much more logical than events recounted by any member of the Stanford family. What *is* likely is that after an excruciating day at the office, after two or three gin and tonics, sometime between 5:40 p.m. and 5:45 p.m., Alan looked up. Outside his kitchen window, facing north, he saw Athalia pull up in her driveway, take a bag of groceries out of the car and rush into her house through the back door.

He slipped out his own back door and got the machete out of the shop. He jumped the three-foot wall separating his house from hers. He went around to the front, rang her doorbell and then he stood against the east wall of her house, shouldering the machete, hidden from her view, waiting. Shortly after, Athalia opened her door. She looked outside. She may have said, "Hello?" Then she shrugged it off and got her little crippled bird Clementine to accompany her as she checked her mail and walked down to the gate to pick up the paper. A neighbor, Charlotte Cooper, peeking out her window, said that she saw her with the little bird gamely hopping behind her. Athalia may have been absorbed in her mail or the newspaper as she walked back to her front steps. By the time she saw Alan, it was too late. She dropped the mail and put her arms up in defense. Alan swung, and the machete hit her on the hand and on the elbow. She tripped, falling backward. Alan came closer, stood over her and chopped eight more times, almost severing her head. The east exterior wall of the house was sprayed with her blood as Alan struck her. He killed her little bird as well.

Alan had snapped. At some point, he came back to himself and stepped slowly back over the concrete wall, trailing blood. In his own backyard, he encountered Patti, standing on the back patio, staring at him. Patricia may have seen him, too, from inside the house. He walked by them toward his car. Patti ran around to the front of the house and put her hand to her mouth. Patricia went upstairs.

Alan staggered to the garage, which was really just an outdoor shed where the family kept the laundry. He grabbed one of Annette's old diapers he used for cleaning his paintbrushes and a dirty towel and rubbed as much blood off as he could. He wrapped the machete in the towel. He got some of his dirty clothes. Then he drove back to work just as he said he did. He got blood on an old sign and on a signpost outside the office. He cleaned up the car. He changed into the dirty clothes from the laundry. He dumped the evidence—the bloodstained clothes, his watch, his tie, his shoes, the machete, the towel and the diaper—on his way home. Alan said he was at the office for twenty minutes, which may have been true. He picked up a textbook and a slide rule. He was home by 7:00 p.m.

There is no way to imagine what he said to Patti to ensure her cooperation, or to Patricia or, later, to Locke or the McCormicks. He may even have considered confessing. In his view, the brutal slaying may have seemed justifiable. But in the end, he decided to ride it out, and his family and his neighbors went along with it. Perhaps they had no choice. Perhaps they were too afraid.

ALIBIS

A few days after the murder, Alan began scouting around for "eyewitnesses" to verify his account that his car was parked at his office between 5:30 p.m. and 6:30 p.m. the night of January 23. Alan actively recruited such testimony. The results were mixed.

Bias creeps into memory without knowledge, without awareness. Carl Tipton, the county worker who found blood on the sign and the signposts next to the county manager's office, swore in a deposition that "Mr. Stanford's car was parked right there where it is usually parked at" between 5:30 p.m. and 6:00 p.m. on January 23. He identified the county seal on the car, as did his companion, Daniel Wilson. They stepped forward to give the information at Alan's request to Frank Upchurch, who was acting unofficially as Alan's lawyer at that point. Two weeks later, they gave the same testimony to Assistant State Attorney Richard Watson, who skillfully disseminated their recollections.

Both men left work at 4:30 p.m. to drive out to the dump off Nine Mile Road, which was about seven or eight miles away. They made a point of stating that Tipton drove "like a snail." They were there for ten or twenty minutes, came back on US 1 and turned by the Road and Bridge Building on their way home. They swore that Alan's car was there between 5:30 p.m. and 6:30 p.m.

Even driving as slowly as possible, it couldn't have been later than 5:20 p.m. when Tipton and Wilson passed Alan's parking spot. More likely, they passed Alan's parking spot while he was still in the building, meeting with Emrich and Murphy.

Floyd Russell Hardin, a heavy equipment operator for the county (and whose sister-in-law, Adelle McLauglin, testified that she saw a strange man in front of Athalia's yard at 4:30 p.m. on the day of the murder), also stepped forward at Alan's request. Floyd Hardin was obligated to Alan Stanford as his employer and because Alan, for some reason, let Floyd reside in a county-owned lighthouse.

Hardin stated that he saw Alan driving on King Street at 6:45 p.m. the night of the murder. He said he waved at Alan, but Alan didn't see him. This sighting proved nothing. Alan could have gone to the county office, cleaned up and been on his way home at that point.

Ray Virgil Fox, a welder with a business on Lewis Speedway near the county complex, was recruited for testimony by Alan and said that he drove by Alan's parking space twice on January 23, at 5:45 p.m. and 6:00 p.m. Both times, Alan's car was there. Fox, who didn't know the names of his employees and couldn't remember how many of them were working for him that day, nevertheless had perfect recall about the precise times and sightings of Alan's car during the crucial half hour between 5:30 p.m. and 6:00 p.m. when Athalia was busy being murdered. However, his recall is wrong. The truck log at Desco Marine shows one entry from Fox Welding on January 23, 1974. Ray signed in at 4:50 p.m. and signed out at 5:20 p.m.

Therefore, he saw Alan's car on the way to the marina at 4:30 p.m. when there was no question that Alan was still at work. Fox said that he left Desco Marine, twenty minutes away on Riberia Street, at 5:30 p.m. He was with a man whose name he thought might be Shorty, and they stopped and bought some beers at a convenience store. He "drove real slow" because of a load of plywood in his truck. As he turned off US 1, he noticed Alan's car parked in front of his office. This time did fit Alan's alibi—it would have been around 5:50 p.m.

The next time he drove past Alan's parking spot that night, on an errand to pick up some steel, he stopped again, got another beer and admitted to Watson that the time could have been "well after 6:00." Watson got Fox to admit that he went to Desco Marine on Tuesday, January 22, and followed the same schedule. But Fox didn't know the time he left the marina on the twenty-second. He couldn't remember if he saw Alan's car that day. It is easier to believe that he had his days mixed up rather than it was only on the twenty-third that his memory functioned, after a fashion, and even that testimony was not strong.

There was much more evidence that Alan's car wasn't where he said it was during the time of the murder. Victor Keiereber, a county employee, swore that he drove by the county manager's office between 5:30 p.m. and 6:00 p.m. on the twenty-third and Stanford's car wasn't there. He remembered the date and time because he went by Bryant Mobile Homes to sign some papers for a house trailer he was buying, and he had an appointment. It was a little after six o'clock when he arrived at Bryant Mobile, one and a half miles south of Stanford's office.

A Mr. Harold Hemmerson, a county employee, stated that on January 23, 1974, he drove by the county manager's office at 6:16 p.m. and noted that Alan's car wasn't there. He was on his way to Jacksonville to visit his stepdaughter, Meredith, who was housed at the Buckner Foundation for unwed mothers. He was logged in at 6:45 p.m. Lieutenant Lightsey checked the log and requested a letter from Mrs. Gay, the executive director, verifying the time. She complied. Both Keiereber and Hemmerson stepped forward because they heard rumors that Alan was at his office at the time of the murder, and they were puzzled because they "went by and he wasn't there."

The day after the murder, Alan went to the mobile home of Lieutenant Charles G. Cannon, which was within walking distance of the county office. He knocked on the door. Cannon was eating supper with his family, but he answered the door. Alan beckoned him outside. Then he asked Cannon if he or his family were home at 6:00 p.m. the previous day. Cannon said that no one in his family was home before 8:30 p.m.

Alan said, "I left home about 5:40 p.m. and came out to the office, arriving about 5:50 p.m. [getting to Lewis Speedway from Marine Street in ten minutes would have been impossible]. It's very important for me to find someone that saw my car in front of my office yesterday afternoon at 6:00 p.m. It was there." Cannon said that he doubted anyone saw anything because the only prisoners there faced the north side of Alan's office and couldn't have seen his car. But he said he'd ask.

Alan said he'd check back with Cannon the following morning. He repeated, "It is very important for me to find someone who saw my car over there at 6:00 p.m. I have several people downtown who saw me driving out this way, but I need to find someone that saw me and my car out here at 6:00 p.m." Then he said, curiously, "I don't know which way they're coming, but I am not the one who did it." He left.

The next day, Cannon was standing with another officer, P.E. McIntire, in front of the jail, watching the county road machine fill in dirt. Alan walked over from his office building around 10:00 a.m. He asked Cannon, "Did you find out anything?"

Cannon said, "No, I did not. I asked the girls upstairs, and they said they were watching TV and saw nothing." Alan asked McIntire if he'd seen Alan's car at 6:00 p.m. McIntire said, no, he'd been off fishing. Alan left. Cannon and McIntire looked at each other. Later, when they reported the incident to Officer Davis, they said that Alan appeared emotional and very nervous. They said he played with his tie and did not seem to be his normal self.

That same day, though, Alan's efforts to establish an alibi bore some fruit. A trustee and inmate in the county jail, Dixon Stanford (no relation to Alan), said, at Alan's request, that he saw Alan's county car on January 23 parked in front of the office "at approximately 7:15–7:30 p.m." This was no help to Alan, but by the time the trial rolled around, Dixon's testimony had changed to "pretty close to 6:30 p.m." In retrospect, it is entirely plausible that Alan's car was at the county office at 6:30 p.m. if Alan came there to clean up and plan where to dispose of the evidence before returning to Marine Street.

By the way, where *was* the evidence?

THE EVIDENCE

*For homicides in which the victim to offender relationship could be identified, 93
percent of female victims…were murdered by a male they knew.*
    −When Men Murder Women *(2012), the Violence Policy Center*

On January 25, 1974, Sheriff Dudley Garrett appeared before Judge
Mathis and issued an affidavit for a search warrant of Alan's home on
126 Marine Street. Garrett wrote, "Affiant believes and has good reason to
believe that in those certain premises…[including the dwelling, the concrete
block fence, the utility shed] there is now being kept on said premises the
following described property: Bloody clothing, cutting instruments, and
many other articles that appear to have blood stains on them."

The search warrant was granted. The officers listed and dated what they
found: tennis shoes in the dryer, some clothing, a shovel and two bloody
concrete blocks. Later, Stanford's lawyer would say the Stanfords weren't
home during the search and that the officers left the house in "complete
disarray." Clearly, the search was thorough. What the officers didn't find
was the murder weapon and bloody clothing they could specifically tie to
the murder. Yet a cursory view of the evidence against Alan Stanford added
up to a very viable suspect. Athalia was publicly threatening his job security.
Alan had made threatening statements to her. Several people could testify
that Athalia was in fear of her life.

Athalia had no real facts to buoy her fear other than threats and petty
vandalism. But other facts were even more frightening. Alan checked out a

machete from the county, presumably to trim some palm fronds. This was not unusual. A lot of people borrowed or owned machetes in Florida in order to tackle the palm fronds and vines indigenous to the region. James Lindsley, a realtor, carried a machete in the trunk of his car to cut away vegetation when he was showing a house. But Lindsley's machete was readily produced, accounted for and dismissed as the murder weapon. It was too small, for one thing. It lacked bloodstains for another. The one that Alan borrowed, however, was mysteriously missing.

David Allen Wehking, a county employee, remembered Freddie Hudnall putting the borrowed knife in the back seat of Alan's county car in December 1973. The machete was eighteen to twenty-eight inches long, and the blade was a few inches wide. The handle was black, and it was fastened to the blade with two brass rivets. The blade showed on the perimeter of the handle.

The Thursday after the murder, Special Agent Herring impounded Alan's car, with the consent of Commissioner Herbie Wiles. Herring released the county car to Randy Diselets at the FDLE Crime Lab in Tallahassee. There was dirt in the trunk of the car that Herring wanted for comparison. Herring wanted to process bloodstains found on the seat and on the steering wheel.

Presented with proof that Alan was a murder suspect, unnerved and desperate to prove his friend's innocence, Herbie had crew chief Freddie Hudnall "pull everything out of his truck" because the machete Alan borrowed was still missing. Alan strolled over and said, "By the way, I returned that machete. I put it back in the truck." But Fred Hudnall said the county had no record of ever getting it back, and he kept an inventory. After Freddie ransacked his truck, the machete was still missing.

Alan pressed the point and met with Hudnell twice, telling him that his refusal to acknowledge the return of the machete was "hurting him." Frank Upchurch Jr. also met with Hudnell and told him he went fishing with Alan "the Sunday after the murder" and that Upchurch said he "sure couldn't picture a man like that doing anything like that, if he did he wouldn't have gone fishing with him." Hudnall said he wanted to help Stanford, but still, the machete was missing. He was sure of it.

Alan's daughter Patricia also gave a detailed account of the machete, which she'd seen in her father's shop but had never seen him use. She said that he told her mother that "he found it some where" and that he was going to "give it to his men out on the Road and Bridge Department when they go out in the woods or something to kill snakes." And, no, it was no longer in his shop.

Left: Eddie Lightsey pointing to a blood spot. *Courtesy of the St. Johns County Sheriff's Department.*

Below: Bloody signpost near Alan's office. *Courtesy of the St. Johns County Sheriff's Department.*

Blood spot on cellophane found near Alan's car. *Courtesy of the St. Johns County Sheriff's Department.*

Then there was the trail of blood leading from the murder scene to the wall of Stanford's yard. There was blood on two concrete blocks found in Alan's garage. There was the drop of blood on cellophane found beside Stanford's parking space and blood on the sign and signposts lying outside the sign shop, which lay between the main road and bridge office where Alan worked and where he may have fled after the murder.

Carl Tipton, an employee of the St. Johns County Road and Bridge Department, the same guy who swore that he saw Alan's car in front of the county office at the time of the murder, testified to Assistant State Attorney Watson that he found the bloody sign and signpost. He speculated to Lieutenant Lightsey that a machete could be hidden in a variety of places around the shop, including unused gas tanks, tar barrels, a steam jenny or a smokestack.

At the same time, Tipton, like many other people who knew Alan Stanford, was convinced that Alan was innocent. Tipton said, "Well, Mr. Stanford is a very funny fellow, you don't figure him out, I can't figure him out…he [Stanford] has always got the same approach just as sure as the morning's going to come he will be the same way; he is cool, he is never radical headed, he is very calm and when he speaks to you it's in a low tone of voice, he has never raised his voice."

To drive the calmness of his demeanor home, Alan Stanford gave an interview to the *St. Augustine Record* a week after the murder. Patrick Lynn, the managing editor, gave him a nice headline: "Stanford: Pressure 'Has Been Enormous.'" Alan admitted to "being angered and frustrated on the inside" and that he knew he was a suspect, but (Lynn emphasized) "the quiet soft-spoken manager didn't betray his feelings outwardly." Alan "was quite aware that I've been a suspect since the day after," but Alan said it had gone on long enough and that he wished the police would stop disrupting his life and focus on finding the real culprit. Alan said if the *Record* "could dispel that idea [that he murdered his neighbor], it would be a real public service." There was no mention of the extent of the tragedy that befell his dead neighbor, no hint of sympathy except for

Stanford: Pressure 'H

By PATRICK LYNN
Managing Editor

If Alan Stanford Jr., is a beleaguered man, he doesn't show it.

Although he admits to being angered and frustrated "on the inside," the quiet, soft-spoken county manager doesn't betray his feelings outwardly.

In an exclusive interview with the Record this morning, Stanford acknowledged that the pressure on him and his family "has been enormous" since the Jan. 23 slaying of his next door neighbor, Mrs. Athalia Ponsell Lindsley.

HE'S BEEN "quite aware that I've been a suspect since the day after," says Stanford, "but now I feel it's gone on long enough and it's time for them (the investigators) to concentrate on other possibilities."

Stanford and his family have been subjected to widespread rumor in St. Johns County and in Jacksonville since the murder.

Rumors have been flying thick and fast about the slaying, and last week it was widely and erroneously circulated in St. Augustine that a Jacksonville radio station reported Stanford's arrest. Two days ago a Jacksonville station broadcast Stanford's

name as one of two suspects in the case, and a Jacksonville newspaper made a similar statement this morning.

"I KNOW I'm under a cloud of suspicion," Stanford told the Record this morning as he shook his head in frustration. "If you could dispel that idea, it would be a public service.

"In the first place," he added, "I have not been accused, and in the second place, if I am accused, it's still only an accusation.

"It's not fair that I should be a suspect of murder indefinitely," added Stanford quietly.

He said he regrets that local lawmen have narrowed the focus of their investigation on him. "While it seems to me the sheriff's office and the local police have been restrained, considerate and

quite f... been q... not aw...

"The vestiga venient...

"I C... attack me, it... there i... study,... one mi...

His public on St meetin Ther Mariu Lindsl she on

ALAN STANFORD

Murder Upsetting, But Most Do Not Fear For Safety

Alan Stanford. "Pressure has been enormous." *Courtesy of the St. Augustine Record.*

himself. Lynn noted that Alan had just "celebrated his birthday." In the accompanying close-up photograph, Alan Stanford was smiling.

Still, there was no hard physical evidence specifically linking Alan to the crime. There was no murder weapon, there was no bloodstained clothing, and after Locke McCormick recanted his eyewitness account, there was no witness. Sheriff Garrett could not arrest a man as socially prominent as Alan Stanford without hard evidence. Alan even passed a polygraph test, administered by a friend of his lawyer friend Frank Upchurch Jr., a Mr. Bud Miller, who worked as a polygraph examiner for Zales Jewelers.

Alan declined taking the lie detector test with Special Agent Joe Townsend of the FDLE, as James Lindsley had done, electing instead for the private sector to determine whether he was lying about the events of January 23. The prosecution spent three weeks trying to get Mr. Miller to return its calls about the results of Alan's polygraph. Finally, the prosecution called his employers, and that did the trick. First, however, Mr. Miller's employers declared emphatically that they had not authorized the polygraph test and that, in fact, administering such tests to anyone other than a Zales employee was against company policy.

In a telephone conversation with Captain Williams, Mr. Miller established that he had fifteen years of experience in his field, ran three tests on Alan and asked about seven or eight questions on each test. He said Alan "checked out" but added, "If for any reason I am wrong or if subsequent investigation reveals me wrong, then all I can say in the matter is, well justice will prevail and it will, it most certainly will."

On Thursday, February 14, 1974, Special Agent Herring and another special agent by the name of Uebelher went to Alan's county office to interview Alan again. Special Agent Herring advised Alan of his rights, and Alan must have realized that law enforcement was not dropping the investigation. Alan said that he wouldn't talk to them anymore unless his friend and lawyer Frank Upchurch was there.

The next day, February 15, 1974, the *St. Augustine Record* ran an editorial on page four headlined, "Common Sense in Wake of Tragedy." The editors bemoaned the fact that "speculation as to whether or not the case has been properly handled by authorities is not yet subjected to comment." They warned, "What some persons perhaps fail to realize is that a murderer could strike a member of their family…to this person or persons, having information concerning the case, but hesitating to come forward due to a desire 'not to become involved' we hasten to point out the age old commandment, 'Thou Shalt Not Kill.'"

Regardless of the pious exhortations of the local newspaper, by mid-February, Sheriff Garrett had nothing. Yet Garrett was known for getting things done. Appointed sheriff by Governor Claude Kirk to replace L.O. Davis, who was removed from office in 1970, Garrett was elected on his own steam in 1972 after putting an end to blatant prostitution, cockfighting and bolita (gambling). A former marine, Garrett was fair but tough, and he closed down bootleggers' stills in St. Johns County that had been around for decades. He instituted twenty-four-hour shifts for law enforcement officers to protect St. Johns County

Sheriff Garrett had something to prove, and he was not a man cowed by the upper echelon in St. Johns County. He wanted to charge the murderer who killed Athalia. But he needed more than he had so far. He searched "forest, fields, swamps," and on January 29, he drained the Maria Sanchez Lake, a watery property at the foot of Cordova Street off Lewis Speedway. He admitted that it was "a shot in the dark" insofar as locating the murder weapon. However, he correctly assumed, along with Dominic Nicklo, that "Mrs. Lindley's slayer may have hurriedly dumped or buried his clothes, presumably blood splattered, and his weapon,

Maria Sanchez Lake. *Photo by Bob Randall.*

Stanford house in 1974. *Courtesy of the St. Johns County Sheriff's Department.*

somewhere in the vicinity of Marine Street." In the Maria Sanchez Lake, however, he found nothing but garbage.

His officers searched the Stanford home, but they failed to find the murder weapon. He put an ad in the *St. Augustine Record*, offering a reward for information leading to the arrest of Athalia's killer. The headline in the February 16–17 weekend edition of the *Record* read, "$500 Offered to Person Finding Murder Weapon." The article headed off with Sheriff Dudley Garrett saying, "The reward is for the recovery of the weapon [used to murder Athalia Ponsell Lindsley] which I believe to be a machete." Then fate smiled on him: he got his evidence the next day.

During Stanford's murder trial, Walter Arnold, lawyer for the defense, made much of the fact that the damning evidence against Alan was found the day after Garrett offered a reward. It seemed too convenient. He thought the way the reward was worded was odd, especially the mention of the machete. He made much of fact that the man who found it, Dewey Lee, was an alcoholic, a man who'd been arrested twice for public drunkenness and an informant for Lieutenant Eddie Lightsey. Dewey Lee was paid $500 in cash, cash he called his "machete award," which the local gossips speculated came through James Lindsley. It looked like a payoff if you didn't know the facts and if you didn't look too closely.

In fact, though, Henry Duward Lee (aka Dewey Lee) was always prowling around junkyards, garbage dumps and the woods looking for things. That was Dewey Lee. He was a hard-luck guy, scavenging what he could. He never got beyond the tenth grade in school, and he'd been divorced twice. He took care of his three kids, aged twenty-two, sixteen and fourteen. A World War II vet, he collected disability for a head injury, but he wasn't one for sitting around. He was a shrimp fisherman with his own boat. He was a mechanic, known for his skill with Fords, and he'd worked in the county garage for twenty years. He hunted automobile parts. He looked for stolen cars and oddities. He looked for his youngest teenage daughter, who had run off and whom he feared was dead. "You know how it is in this day and age," he said sadly. And, yes, he was friendly with Eddie Lightsey, who probably told him to keep an eye out for the Marine Street murder weapon, specifically a machete. Dewey spent two weeks looking. First, he took his dog and looked in the woods five miles north of Highway 1. Nothing. So Dewey started thinking. During his deposition, he recalled:

> *I figured it wasn't in the lake* [Maria Sanchez], *they pumped the lake. It had to be in an out of the way place where nobody could see. I just drove until I got to that particular spot. Drove down right near the water of Lake Sanchez. Went to the garbage dump. Parked the car on this old road that goes down into the dump. Riberia Street. It's marshy, the San Sebastian river, after you leave Riberia Street. It runs through a marshy area—it's three fourths of a mile to the first place you can even get to the river, on the west bank.*

Dewey Lee walked the marsh at the south end of Ribera Street at low tide. Riberia Street was only a few miles from Marine Street. It didn't take a genius to figure out that a river used as a dump was a logical place to dispose of the accouterments of murder—that is, if you had the stomach for it. Eddie Roy Lightsey may have even suggested the spot to Dewey Lee as worthy of investigation.

The two men had much in common. Lieutenant Lightsey was a self-made man from Georgia with little formal education but with a dogged, thorough way about him in an investigation. A dragline operator for the Road and Bridge Department before he worked for the sheriff's office, he was a canny man with street smarts and little use for Alan Stanford, who'd fired his son from his job with the Road and Bridge Department.

Sunday, though, was his day to sleep in. When Dewey Lee called Lightsey at home on Sunday, February 17, 1974, at about 10:00 a.m. from an office telephone at the St. Augustine Boatyard, the Lightseys let the phone ring. At 10:45 a.m., the phone rang again. Eddie instructed his wife, "Say I ain't home or something."

Eddie's wife answered the phone. She listened. Then with her hand over the receiver, she told her husband, "Eddie, Dewey Lee is on the telephone and says he has got something important he wants to see you about."

Eddie picked up the receiver and said, "Hello?"

Dewey said, "Eddie?"

"Yes."

"I been trying to get a hold of you about 45 minutes. I got something I think you ought to see."

"You have?"

"Yeah." Dewey said. "How about coming on and meeting me at the end of Riberia Street?"

Eddie said, "Okay Dewey." Eddie showed up with his son, nicknamed "Little Lightsey," about fifteen minutes later. They went to the small creek west of the sewer treatment plant at the foot of Riberia Street.

Dewey said, "I got something down here you ought to look at. It might mean something." Eddie followed him over to a high bank and slid down to the marsh. "Look over there," Dewey said. Dewey pointed toward a machete, seventeen feet away from the base of the bank, "laying down there all rusted up, turned upside down, the blade facing up." Next to it was a pile of mud, but peeking through the top was what looked like something rolled up in a towel, a pink towel with a belt hanging half out of it.

Eddie said, "Doggone, that looks like it might be a machete, stuff and clothes we're looking for." Eddie and Dewey threw some loose boards out in the muck because the tide was out and the ground was low. Eddie got as far as the machete, but he had his good shoes on and couldn't reach it, mired as it was in muck. He said to "Little Lightsey," "Son, do me a favor, just pick that machete up by the tip end, just by the tip end. There might be some prints or something we can get off of it, pick it up by the tip end, turn around and hand it to me." The boy did as he was told, and Eddie walked back down the plank to the shore and laid the machete gently down on the bank.

Dewey got a long board, scooped up the towel and swung it around. Eddie and his son picked up the other end of the board, and the men

The evidence found in the swamp by the city dump off Riberia Street. *Courtesy of the St. Johns County Sheriff's Department.*

Machete entered as evidence—the murder weapon. *Courtesy of the St. Johns County Sheriff's Department.*

walked ashore and set the board down with the towel dangling on the end. Dewey and Little Lightsey watched as Eddie opened up the bloodstained towel. Unrolled, the towel contained a Hamilton wristwatch whose face was stained with blood, a pair of dark-blue pants with blood on one of the pants legs, one long-sleeved white shirt "pretty well saturated with blood stains," a white handkerchief, a baby diaper with blue paint on it, a black belt and a purple tie. Everything was soaking wet. There was some blond hair on the trousers and on the machete. Lightsey took Polaroid pictures.

Sometime after 11:00 a.m., Deputy Sheriff Robert Williams got a call from Lieutenant Eddie Lightsey directing him to the St. Augustine landfill located at the south end of Riberia Street. Deputy Williams found a black wingtip shoe in the marsh. The following day, Deputy Williams brought Dixon Stanford, the trustee from the county jail, and another inmate to search the marsh. They found the other shoe.

It would be interesting to speculate what Alan Stanford Jr. wore for shoes when he arrived back home around 7:00 p.m. on the night of the murder, January 23. If the bloodstained wingtip shoes in the marsh were really his, he would have arrived home in his stocking feet. Given the distraction of the murder investigation, it was unlikely that anyone noticed.

The evidence from the marsh was sealed up and sent to the FDLE lab in Tallahassee. When it came back, it was locked in an evidence room made of coquina rock at the back of Garrett's office beyond the photo lab in the courthouse. Five days later, on Friday, February 22, 1974, Sheriff Garrett issued a warrant for Alan's arrest. The charge was first-degree murder.

THE ARREST AND THE INDICTMENT

A tragic, tragic thing has happened. A poor, poor man was wrongfully accused.
—Herbie Wiles

Special Agent Dallas Herring found a serial number and special markings on the bloodstained Hamilton watch recovered from the marsh of the San Sebastian River. The jeweler, Charles Tanner of Phinney Tanner, who repaired it for Stanford, could identify the numbers and letters. That wasn't all.

In addition, Lieutenant Lightsey could definitively prove, through Bank Americard purchases, that Patricia Stanford purchased the trousers found in the marsh of the San Sebastian River at Kixie Clothing Store. In fact, Assistant State Attorney Richard Watson depositioned a Mr. Kenneth Henry Beeson Jr., a tailor from the store, who swore that he sold the pants to Patti on June 16, 1973. Watson asked, "Are these exactly like the trousers you sold Mrs. Stanford?"

Beeson said, "I wish I could say no but they are, I am afraid I remember selling her that pattern." He sold her the shirt, too, Alan's size, 15¾, and he had the credit card receipt to prove it. In addition, there was a laundry mark from Zoric Cleaners on the bloodstained shirt, which definitively proved that it belonged to Alan.

Lieutenant Lightsey was even able to prove—again through credit card receipts—that the blue- and tangerine-colored paint on the bloodstained diaper found in the San Sebastian River exactly matched paint that Alan bought two years ago at Sherwin Williams with a

Alan Stanford Arrest Ends Murder Suspense

By PATRICK LYNN
Managing Editor

Four weeks of anxiety and rumor in the wake of the slaying of Mrs. Athalia Ponsell Lindsley ended last night, quietly and without drama, with the arrest of Alan G. Stanford Jr.

The 49-year-old county manager, known for his quiet demeanor and self control, betrayed no emotion when he was arrested at his home.

SHERIFF Dudley Garrett, police Sgt. Dominic Nicklo and one unidentified agent of the Florida Department of Law Enforcement made the arrest.

Armed with an arrest warrant signed by

County Judge Charles Mathis, the three lawmen drove to the two-story Spanish-style Stanford home at 136 Marine Street.

A ring of the doorbell went unanswered so the three men went to the rear yard where the Stanfords, Alan, his wife Patricia, and their three-year-old daughter were gathered.

Sheriff Garrett motioned Stanford aside to explain their presence. At that point, Stanford invited the lawmen inside to the kitchen where the formal arrest was made.

Sheriff Garrett read the arrest warrant and officer Nicko followed with a reading of Stanford's civil rights.

STANFORD volunteered no statements, according to the lawmen, but immediately attempted to contact his attorney, Frank D. Upchurch Jr., by phone.

There was no response. Upchurch was out of town on a sailing trip. To accommodate Stanford's request for counsel, Sheriff Garrett dispatched a patrol car to the ranch of Hamilton Upchurch, the brother and law partner of Frank Upchurch Jr.

Meanwhile, Stanford was whisked to the county courthouse and within an hour was before Judge Mathis for a first hearing. An arraignment has been set for Tuesday morning when Stanford will be asked how he pleads to the charge of murder in the first degree.

AS OF NOON Saturday, Stanford was still being held in the county jail without bail. He received a visit at 9:30 Friday night from his wife but he declined to see a

reporter from The Record.

Still shrouded in a cloak of silence is the evidence on which Stanford was arrested.

Sheriff Garrett, who carried the brunt of the investigation, was close-mouthed about the case last night.

Asked if he had found the machete which is the presumed murder weapon, Sheriff Garrett replied: "I can't comment on that."

Asked if he had uncovered any "hard" evidence or found an eyewitness to the slaying, the sheriff responded:

"I CAN'T answer any of these questions. I'm probably going to wind up in court as a witness so I can't discuss the case."

Garrett's reluctance to discuss the case for legal reasons even extended to his family. His son-in-law, Ron Sachs, a reporter for the Miami Herald, called for information about the case. "He got the same treatment, I told him I couldn't give him anything."

The sheriff only allowed as how he had enough evidence to convince the state attorney's office that he had sufficient evidence to warrant Stanford's arrest.

The murder was particularly brutal, even veteran police officers who were stunned by ferocity of the crime.

Police Chief Virgil Stuart, reacting by stating that it was "pretty brutal, the worst I can recall right now."

Stuart also stated the only possible motive was: "Hate, just pure hate! That's just speculation on my part." However, less than 10 days later the city police chief was quoted as saying, "the trail is cold,

ALAN STANFORD

Alan Stanford is arrested. *Courtesy of the St. Augustine Record.*

STANFORD GRANTED $20,000 BOND AFTER ENTERING INNOCENT PLEA

By PATRICK LYNN
Managing Editor
Smiling slightly and apparently in good

spirits, County Manager Alan G. Stanford Jr. pleaded not guilty to the charge of first degree murder in county court this morning and was granted $20,000 bond.

THE ARRAIGNMENT took six minutes as a crowded courtroom of newsmen,

neighbors, friends and family looked on.

His wife Patricia and their teenage daughter, Patti, sat quietly among the spectators and joined Stanford in a subdued room after the brief court appearance.

Stanford, wearing a tan business suit, was taken from the county jail shortly before 10 a.m. and entered the courtroom at 10:20, nodding and smiling to his wife and daughter seated in the front row.

Appearing for the prosecution was Richard D. Watson, assistant state attorney, who read the formal charges: "The state charges you with unlawfully killing Athalia Ponsell Lindsley on Jan. 23 with a knife, commonly known as a machete."

Asked by County Judge Charles Mathis how he pleaded to the charge, Stanford's attorney Frank D. Upchurch Jr., said:

"Mr. Stanford enters a plea of not guilty."

UNEMPLOYED in the first court hearing was the matter of a preliminary trial at which the state would present evidence against the accused. Upchurch urged a delay in setting the preliminary trial "because we are now contacting an attorney who specializes in these matters."

Upchurch said he hoped to enlist the services of an attorney this afternoon, whereupon Judge Mathis asked Upchurch and Watson to agree on a date for a preliminary hearing.

Both attorneys agreed to waive the requirement of a preliminary hearing to be held within seven days of the arraignment.

Watson said he needed additional time to convene the St. Johns County Grand Jury to hear the evidence against Stanford. He also needed time, he said, to arrange for the appearance of state crime laboratory specialists to present information in the case.

THE $20,000 BAIL was granted by Judge Mathis "with some reluctance."

"I prefer not to set a bond in this case," Judge Mathis replied to a bond request by Upchurch.

But Upchurch said the fact that Stanford is in jail "complicates communication."

"Is he stable?" asked Judge Mathis.

"Yes, sir," replied Upchurch. "He has been a prime suspect to this thing since the beginning and has made no attempt to leave town. He has been responsive to any request I've had to, but his friends have

offered to come forward to post bond," replied Upchurch.

Assistant state attorney Watson expressed a preference against granting any bail in the matter, and said to the judge:

"If you set bond, I request that it not be less than $50,000."

THE JUDGE APPEARED to waver, setting bond at $20,000.

The formal proceedings finished, Stanford, his attorney, his family and his pastor, Rev. Michael Ross, gathered in a

small room off the courtroom.

A short time later, he was returned to the county jail from the rear of the courthouse under the glare of revolving cameras and waiting newsmen.

At the jail, Stanford paused by the main entrance to respond to questions by the press. (See related story, Page One)

Meanwhile, friends of the Stanford family were arranging the $20,000 bond. Stanford was expected to be released this afternoon.

Record Photo by PHILIP WHITLEY

Chief Jailer Charles Cannon, Stanford Arrive At Courthouse For Arraignment

'Five Eyewitnesses Saw Me At Office' --Stanford

ing that he is resolved to "see this through," County Manager Alan G. Stanford Jr., this morning reaffirmed his

them and he wanted to be sure they were through.

"AS IT TURNED out, the caretaker was

ASKED HOW he got along with Mrs. Ponsell Lindsley, a neighbor, Stanford said there was "practically no con-

The St. Augustine RECORD

"SERVING ST. JOHNS COUNTY AND THE NATION'S OLDEST CITY SINCE 1894"

VOL. LXXIII No. 175   Tuesday, February 26, 1974   Ten Cents Per Copy

Alan Stanford smiling as he alights in handcuffs on the day of his arrest. *Courtesy of the St. Augustine Record.*

credit card. Trace elements of the paints were compared and were considered indistinguishable.

Special Agent Dallas Herring, Sheriff Dudley Garrett and Sergeant Dominic Nicklo arrested Alan Griffith Stanford Jr. around 5:00 p.m. at his home on Friday, February 22. Alan consequently spent the weekend in jail. There is a picture of him on the front page of the *St. Augustine Record* stepping out of the police van in handcuffs with a broad and genial smile on his face.

Anne Heymen, a reporter at the *St. Augustine Record*, said that she remembered the day Alan was arrested because "all the junior league girls were crying." In fact, public sympathy quickly coalesced on Alan's side. The Stanfords were a prominent and popular family in St. John's County. Either people didn't believe Alan committed murder or they thought Athalia had it coming.

Patrick Lynn, managing editor for the *St. Augustine Record*, wrote a two-column article on the front page headlined, "Alan Stanford Arrest Ends Murder Suspense." To the discerning reader, it did not help Alan's case. It contained lines such as, "The 48 year old county manager known for his quiet demeanor and self control betrayed no emotion when he was arrested at his home." Who wouldn't be upset about an arrest for first-degree murder in front of wife, children and neighbors? Then, amazingly, Lynn drew an incongruous comparison of Sheriff Garrett and Alan Stanford as though the lawman and the alleged murderer were equals: "Like Stanford, Sheriff Garrett is a low-key individual. The two men share much in common. Both are quiet, soft-spoken, more eager to discuss than debate. Neither is given to extravagant emotion or speech. Both men would prefer to listen rather than talk, both prefer to read faces, accept well-meaning advice politely, and handle people with deference."

Later, in an "Across the Desk" column (which was basically gossip), *Record* editor Hoopie Tebault made sure that readers knew how to contribute to Alan's "income supplement fund," which his pastor, Michael Boss at Trinity Episcopal, organized for him. Tebault chatted in her column that Alan came by to thank her for the "fair manner" in which the *Record* presented his case. When James Lindsley came by to "express a dim view of the coverage of the case" and Managing Editor Lynn's shabby portrayal of Athalia versus his sympathetic takes on Alan, Tebault explained, "It is most difficult to obtain information from the state...Prosecutors and police are 'tightlipped' and the only source of information in a case of this nature comes from the defendant."

Of course, if Tebault's explanation held any water, smiling faces of accused murderers would adorn every issue of the *Record*, and Tebault would advocate fundraising on all of their behalves. Small wonder that assistant state attorney and prosecutor Richard Watson lambasted Tebault, Lynn, Feagin and Powell for "making it impossible to have an unbiased trial."

But on the weekend of February 22, 1974, Alan was in jail, where lawmakers believed he belonged. Frank Upchurch Jr. visited Alan a few times that weekend. Frank came from an "old Florida" family, hailing from Fernandina Beach and from a long line of lawyers and judges. He was a father, a husband, a man with a sterling reputation, a World War II pilot and a veteran who saw active duty in the Pacific. He was fairly characterized in the newspaper as a man "active in many local, county and state organizations, serving in official capacities with a splendid record of achievement in activities for the betterment of the area and its people." He was one of the few men who tried to negotiate with civil rights activists on a level playing field during the racial turmoil that roiled St. Augustine during the 1960s.

Frank sincerely believed that Alan was innocent, and he knew his friend was in trouble. Frank agreed to represent Alan during the murder trial, but he recommended Alan find a criminal city lawyer from Jacksonville or Orlando. It turned out to be good advice.

In fact, the most pressing and immediate problem facing Alan that last weekend of February 1974, a month after his neighbor was slaughtered on her front steps, was finding a criminal lawyer and raising bail money so that he could get out of jail on Monday. Curiously, he didn't take out a lien on his home at 126 Marine Street, although it was surely worth at least $100,000. Were there, in fact, real questions about Alan's money management skills? Did they lend some credence to the charges of kickbacks that Athalia kept pursuing?

In order to raise money for his defense, Alan needed to get out of jail, and with a capital murder charge pending, even that was questionable. Alan assumed his most ingratiating persona. His hearing was set for 10:00 a.m., Monday, February 25, 1974. "Smiling slightly and apparently in good spirits," Alan, via Frank Upchurch Jr., pleaded "not guilty" to the formal charge of first-degree murder read by Assistant State Attorney Richard Watson as "the unlawful killing of Athalia Ponsell Lindsley with a knife, commonly known as a machete." The arraignment took six minutes in a crowded courtroom. Patti and Patricia Stanford sat in the front row.

The bail was set at $20,000. There was some question about releasing a man into the community after he was charged with a capital murder offense. Judge Mathis said, "I prefer not to set a bond in this case." He meant it. This was the same judge who, ten years earlier, had sent the "St. Augustine Four"—four black teenagers—to adult prison and then to reform school because they refused to sign a paper saying they would cease civil rights demonstrations after being arrested for ordering lunch at the local Woolworths.

Upchurch complained that keeping Alan in jail would "complicate communication." Mathis asked if Alan was stable. Upchurch said, "Yes sir. He has been a prime suspect in this thing since the beginning and he has made no attempt to leave town. He has been responsive to any request. In fact, his friends have offered to come forward to post bail."

In fact, his wife, Patti, and one friend of the family, Jennings C. Dumas (godfather of Patricia), pledged stock shares as collateral for Alan's bond. Patti undoubtedly acquired the stocks from her father, Perry, as events later in life proved. Later, Stanford, his family and Pastor Michael Boss of Trinity Episcopal Church gathered in a small room off the courtroom. Then Alan was escorted out the back door of the courthouse and back to the county jail to await his release.

Allowed to pause in front of the jail, Alan made a statement for the press: "Five eyewitnesses saw me at my office that evening." In fact, no one saw Alan at his office that evening. His secretary, Hazel McCallum, and his technical clerk, Jody Hough, left at least forty minutes before he did. Some unreliable witnesses claimed to have seen Alan's car parked in front of his office on January 23, but most of the sightings were well off the time of the actual murder, which took place close to 6:00 p.m.

Then Alan averred to the press and to the public that he had practically no contact, ever, with Athalia, which documented public records could easily prove was far from the truth. The *Record* didn't check the facts and just printed what Alan said. He wasn't released from jail until 8:00 p.m., but Alan put the time to good use, interviewing lawyers, visiting with Patricia and with Perry Mullen, who was a loyal yet, as it turned out, foresighted father-in-law.

Alan's last visitor was Commissioner Herbie Wiles, who, curiously, cited the purpose of his visit as "business" and did not add "friend" to the title column. It was Herbie's second visit. He came in the morning on Saturday, February 23, and stayed for an hour. The visit on Monday was nearly as long. Since Alan was facing a grand jury indictment, it is not hard to discern what Herbie's purpose may have been.

Earlier that day, a special meeting of the Board of County Commissioners of St. Johns County was held at 2:00 p.m. in the county courthouse. Alan was still in jail, but he sent a letter dated February 24 to the commission and directed to the attention of "Hon. Herbert L. Wiles, Chairman." The letter read as follows:

Gentlemen:

As you are aware, I have been arrested and charged with a serious crime and a crime, which I assure you I did not commit. While I can ill afford the loss of income at this time, I do not feel that I could expect to continue my duties with the county while I stand accused.

Therefore, I request that I be granted a leave of absence for an indefinite period of time until final disposition of the pending charges.

Yours very truly,
Alan G. Stanford, Jr.

According to the minutes of the meeting, Attorney Willard Howatt advised that the only other alternative was to suspend Alan. Actually, that was not the only alternative. They could have fired him. Not spoken, but surmised, was the probability of a lawsuit if Alan was acquitted of all charges. Howatt said that there was nothing "legally wrong with granting an indefinite leave of absence but would not go so far as saying until disposition of the case." The commissioners unanimously carried a motion to grant Alan G. Stanford Jr. a leave of absence for an indefinite period without pay.

Pete Hardeman, who had served as the interim county manager until Alan was hired two years earlier, was temporarily appointed to the position once again and given a $3,600 raise, which made his salary a little over half of what Alan was earning before his leave. Alan's first order of business as a county manager in 1972 was to turn down Hardeman's request for a raise. Then he tried, without success, to fire him. Now Alan Stanford was gone. The irony may have pleased Hardeman, who was no fan of the former county manager.

The grand jury indictment was held on March 1, 1974. That night, a Sergeant Bandy went to Alan's home to serve Alan with the capias. Alan was on the phone with Frank Upchurch when Bandy arrived, and he made the police officer cool his heels in the living room for five minutes before he got off the phone. Then Bandy read Alan his rights and officially indicted him for murder in the first degree. Bandy noted that Alan was "understanding" and "did not seem upset."

The prosecutor's case looked unshakably firm. They had death threats, a motive, a murder weapon and Alan's bloodstained clothes and his watch. The blond hairs on the trousers and on the machete proved to be Athalia's. They had testimony from Alan, his daughter and his wife that was contradictory and strayed far from the verifiable facts of the case. True, Locke McCormick rescinded his eyewitness testimony, but they could still get him on the stand and establish some culpability toward Alan. James Lindsley had a solid alibi, and there was no other viable suspect. As the state attorney's widow, Sally Boyles, said forty-one years later, "People don't fly in and chop somebody's head off and fly off into the sunset."

They had worked hard to assemble their evidence to catch the killer in their midst. And they had done a damned good job. Sheriff Dudley Garrett; detective Dominic Nicklo; the lead investigators, Eddie Lightsey and Robert Williams; Special Agent Dallas Herring; Assistant State Attorney Richard Watson; and the state attorney, Steven Boyles, must have felt pretty smug the day the grand jury indictment came down. They had their man. What could possibly go wrong?

Enter Walter Arnold Jr.

THE DEFENSE

Really and truly, the most vital one on the case was Alan's lawyer.
—Philip Whitley

Walter Arnold Jr. was a self-made man. He was a graduate of Jacksonville's Andrew Jackson High School, a scholarship student at the University of Florida and a captain on a navy gunboat during World War II. He was also a man with some of his own demons. He was a second son, and his mother and father divorced when he was only five. Like many families after a divorce, he, his mother and his siblings were thereafter doomed to a life of poverty, although his father was still well off. Walter sought father figures as a youth and as a young man, and he fortunately found them: his vice-principal, Earl Lehman, at Andrew Jackson High School and Mr. Julian Fant, a county attorney for Duval County and his first boss. These men mentored and encouraged him. Walter Arnold never felt that he was brilliant or above average in intelligence. He made up for these perceived limitations with grit and hard work.

By the time 1974 rolled around, Walter was sixty-three years old and a partner in Arnold, Stratford and Booth, a prestigious law firm in Jacksonville. Arnold, Stratford and Booth were all related by blood or by marriage, and they specialized in criminal and in eminent domain cases. They were good at it, and they very rarely lost. Walter Arnold was the alpha lawyer in this small, discerning partnership. A self-described loner and an independent man, Walter cared less about money than he did about accepting cases that, in his words, "were interesting to me." He was a hands-on lawyer, and he rarely delegated any responsibilities. In his own words, "In the majority of cases I tried, I knew more about the case than anyone else in the courtroom."

Based on Frank Upchurch's recommendation, Alan hired Arnold, Stratford and Booth on February 25, although they didn't become active in the case until after the grand jury indictment in March. Of course, Alan

Trinity Episcopal. *Photo by Bob Randall.*

didn't have the money to hire them himself. Instead, his father-in-law, Perry Mullen, a reporter, editor and executive for the Associated Press, reached into his deep pockets and provided the hefty retainer.

Alan wasn't working, Patti didn't work and they apparently had no savings in spite of Alan's high salary. Walter Arnold delicately phrased Alan's dilemma as, "He was not in very good financial circumstances." So, Pastor Michael Boss of Trinity Episcopal dove into fundraising and provided money for the Stanfords to live on in the year preceding the murder trial. In retrospect, it is astounding that a religious organization would sponsor, as charity, an accused murderer.

Trinity Episcopal Church was a spired structure smack in the middle of town on the corner of King and St. George Streets. It was across the street from James Lindsey's real estate office. James and Athalia did not attend the church—in fact, they were married at a local Presbyterian church even though Athalia had been an Episcopalian all her life.

Trinity Episcopal had a checkered history and a barred door to outsiders of St. Augustine. Catering to an upper- and a middle-class congregation, many of whom could trace their ancestry back to the British conquest of St. Augustine, its members were unanimously white collar and white skinned. During the civil rights demonstrations in St. Augustine in the 1960s, members of Trinity Episcopal actually shut and locked the doors in the faces of prospective black worshippers accompanied by Mrs. Peabody, a civil rights activist and the mother of the governor of Massachusetts. Trinity's refusal to seat citizens of color made the news all over the nation, including articles in the *New York Times*. Martin Luther King Jr. said, "It is appalling that the most segregated hour of Christian America is eleven o'clock on Sunday morning."

The vestrymen were primarily responsible for this unchristian response to new parishioners of color. In ensuing weeks, black residents of St. Augustine were unceremoniously ousted when they dared to pass the threshold into the halls of this particular house of worship. Their bishop had to threaten the Trinity vestrymen with excommunication before they backed down. A former reverend, Charles Seymour, said, "There was a certain built-in selfishness about the people in Trinity. They were satisfied with themselves and what they had and not too concerned about outside."

Ten years later, nothing had changed. St. Augustine insiders, and the Stanford family, gravitated to Trinity Episcopal. Alan joined the ignoble lineage of vestrymen there—after all, he'd been an Episcopal vestryman when he lived in Maryland and in Atlanta too.

Pastor Michael Boss faced criticism from some of the Trinity congregation and from many level-headed non-congregant citizens in St. Johns County. In a letter, James Lindsley accused Boss and the Episcopal Diocese of "[t]hinking it more proper to pray for the wolf than for the slaughtered lamb." Nevertheless, sympathy for the Stanfords and for Alan in particular accrued. Commissioner Herbie Wiles led off the invocation to a commission meeting with a prayer for Alan Stanford.

Meanwhile, Walter Arnold Jr. took charge of the case against Alan. Immediately, he initiated a flurry of motions, which must have astounded Watson, Garrett and Boyles. First, he tried to throw out the grand jury indictment. Then he motioned to suppress the evidence taken from Alan's Marine Street home via the search warrant. He fought Watson's request for a change of venue to Volusia County for the trial. He inspected the jury lists. The court denied his motion to dismiss the indictment, but Arnold won the other battles.

On March 24, 1974, according to records, Arnold filed the motion to suppress the evidence seized from Alan's home as per Garrett's January 25 search warrant. This included the brown shoes, blue jacket, gray work pants, shovel, a bloodstained napkin and two bloodstained concrete blocks. Arnold petitioned to suppress "any tests or experiments made on the items seized and any other evidence obtained as fruits of the items seized."

Arnold claimed that the search warrant violated Alan's constitutional rights. He cited the Fourth Amendment—probable cause—and said that the search warrant did not "set forth sufficient facts to establish probable cause." Since Garrett clearly stated in the search warrant that he was looking for "bloody clothes" in connection with committing a felony, this item sounds dubious.

But Arnold wasn't through. He said the affidavit was not sworn to before the issuing magistrate. He said the affidavit "fails to describe with particularity the place to be searched." Beyond Alan's address and "the dwelling, the concrete block fence, the utility shed," it is true that Garrett did not include a room-by-room description of his intent to search. He said the affidavit did not sufficiently describe the property to be seized. Garrett's description of "bloody clothing, cutting instruments, and many other articles that appear to have blood stains on them" was, in Arnold's estimate, insufficient.

There was minutia in the motion: Garrett didn't bring the seized evidence before the court, and the warrant wasn't issued in duplicate. Arnold concluded that the evidence obtained was the result of an "unlawful search and seizure." Mathis was not the judge in charge of the murder trial. The new judge, Eugene Eastmoore, was in his mid-forties, and he had been a judge for barely a year. He was a competent man, though, and he quickly recognized that Walter Arnold was a force to be reckoned with. He could not deny the thoroughness of Arnold's motions. That included a rebuttal, against Watson, the assistant state attorney, for a change of venue. In retrospect, it sounds odd that the prosecuting attorneys desperately wanted to try a St. Johns County murder case in Volusia, Flagler or Clay County. Usually, the *defense attorney* argued that potential local jurists were hopelessly prejudiced by their proximity to the case.

All that was true about the murder case brought against Alan Stanford. But in his case, it worked in his favor and against the interests of the prosecution hoping to prove Alan guilty. Public sympathy in St. Augustine was in Alan's corner. So, on April 16, 1974, Assistant State Attorney Richard Watson filed a motion for a change of venue for Alan's murder trial. He wrote, "A fair and impartial trial cannot be had in the county where the case is pending." His request was reasonable. After all, Alan was the county manager at the time of the crime, and he was well known throughout St. Johns County. The media coverage was extensive in both the *Florida Times-Union* and, of course, the *St. Augustine Record*. There was also television coverage.

Watson wrote:

> *The publicity of the case, the position of the defendant in County government, the sympathy engendered by prayers being said in public worship, public meetings, defendant's exculpatory statements in the press and television and the fund raising activities has engendered widespread hostility toward the State of Florida and the deceased with the result that it has become impractical and psychologically impossible to select an impartial jury in the county.*

Officer Francis O'Loughlin submitted a signed statement in support of Watson's motion:

> *There exists in St. Johns County, Florida, widespread hostility toward the state of Florida to the extent it is impractical to attempt to seat a jury in St. Johns County, Florida. The publicity surrounding the case and fund raising efforts for the Defendant has prejudiced the public against the deceased and against the State of Florida. I do not believe a jury will be able to base a verdict on the evidence.*

Nancy Powell—managing bureau editor for the *Florida Times-Union*, a friend of Athalia, a member of Trinity Episcopal and the future author of

Bloody Sunset, the fictionalized version of her friend's murder—submitted a sworn statement on Watson's behalf. It read, "My name is Nancy Powell and I reside in St. Johns County, Florida. I am particularly concerned with the number of people donating to the 'defense fund' of the Defendant and feel that any attempt to seat an unbiased jury in St. Johns County, Florida would be impossible."

Their reasoning, of course, was that it would be impossible to select a full jury without one or more panelists concealing the fact that he or she provided some financial support to the Stanford family through the blatant solicitation of funds for that purpose from religious pulpits, public office and the media.

Before the end of April, Walter Arnold responded with a "Traverse and Answer to State's Motion for Change of Venue." In it, Arnold conceded every motion Watson made except for the seating of an impartial jury. He wrote, "The Defendant says there are many hundreds of citizens of St. Johns County, Florida, eligible for jury duty in said county who have not formed or expressed any opinion concerning the guilt or innocence of himself upon the charges now pending against said Defendant in this cause. Moreover, it will be practical to obtain a fair, impartial and qualified jury in St. Johns County, Florida to try this case."

Judge Eastmoore lived in Palatka, Florida, which is in Putnam County. Although Athalia's murder received national coverage, the social intricacies of the community atmosphere and its context would escape anyone who did not live in St. Johns County. Furthermore, it would be expensive and organizationally challenging to change the venue of the trial. Walter Arnold gave Judge Eastmoore a legal loophole to slip through. He took Watson's motion for a change of venue "under advisement" until the trial. He wanted to see if an "impartial" jury could be seated. Potential jurists were not about to admit inherent prejudice. Eastmoore's ruling meant that Arnold won.

Arnold filed several motions "asking for discoveries, such as a bill of particulars and the production of the evidence which the State intended to use against Alan." There was more wrangling over legal technicalities, depositions were taken and research accrued. The trial date was delayed several times, which worked in Arnold's favor as he fine-tuned his defense tactics. Months passed. There was nothing to do but wait.

FRANCES BEMIS

And what rough beast, its hour come round at last,
Slouches towards Bethlehem to be born?

—*W.B. Yates*

The year 1974 was a bad one for retired career women of a certain age who lived on Marine Street. Shortly after Halloween, another horrible murder occurred in St. Augustine. The victim was seventy-six-year-old Frances Bemis, a Marine Street resident and an acquaintance of Athalia's. Frances was killed during her nightly walk, a walk she did not fear even after Athalia was nearly decapitated. On February 1, 1974, she was the neighbor quoted by Jackie Feagin in the *St. Augustine Record* who said, "I think St. Augustine is the safest place I have ever lived in."

If someone was out to get Frances, she was clearly not aware of it. Frances had a wide circle of friends and interests, but she was no one's enemy. Her neighbor Jean Troemel, who accompanied Frances to meetings at art galleries, thought that the murderer "was a renter with a room in the back of Frances's house." Gossip, however, immediately provided a connection between the murders of Athalia and of Frances. Frances "knew" something or she "saw" something related to Athalia's murder, and Frances was about to come forward. Could it be true? An eighty-year-old neighbor, Mrs. Kathleen Shropshire, made a formal statement, saying that Frances often stopped by her house on her nightly walks to chat. Mrs. Shropshire said that Frances told her, "I am sure Alan

Stanford killed Mrs. Lindsley. I know a man that knows something. I am trying to get him to go to the law."

Mrs. Shropshire claimed that on the night of the Bemis murder, November 3, 1974, when she was out walking her dog, "She heard a car door slam and she was watching her dog when she looked up and saw a man on the sidewalk walking fast down the path going towards Marine Street. The man was dressed in a dark suit and Mrs. Shropshire was sure the man was Alan Stanford. It was close to 7:00 p.m."

Mrs. Shropshire, a member of Trinity Episcopal, had contributed to Alan Stanford's defense fund. She clearly was not prejudiced against him. Yet Athalia's murder was in January, and Frances was killed ten months later. If Frances knew something, what was she waiting for? Frances Bemis was not a retiring or a shy woman. She was vibrant, scholarly, social and as healthy as a horse. She did, after all, walk miles every night. She could have lived many more healthy years.

Gossip quickly filled in gaps. To this day, blogs, chat rooms and published accounts are filled with innuendo. Apparently, Frances was writing a book, and in the book, the identity of Athalia's murderer was revealed. There was another eyewitness, and Frances knew who it was.

Was Frances a threat to a murderer's identity? Frances was not subpoenaed as a witness in Alan's upcoming murder trial, either for the prosecution or for the defense. It was true that she was no fan of Alan Stanford, and her sympathies clearly lay in Athalia's court; this did single her out from the common herd of gossipmongers. Still, her opinions were her own, and although she was a professional writer who was occasionally published on the op-ed pages of the *Record*, she had not written a word about the murder. Regarding Athalia's demise and probable suspects, she confined her insights to a small circle of friends. In fact, she barely knew Athalia, and Frances never interacted with Alan except to ask him to stop letting his dog roam the neighborhood unleashed. Alan told her to mind her own business. (This was before the time that he, his wife and his neighbors the McCormicks prosecuted Athalia in court because her barking dogs were such a nuisance.)

Still, there was no doubting the strangeness and the innate violence characterizing the murders of Frances and Athalia. It seemed like more than a coincidence. Frances and Athalia had so much in common. Both women forged successful careers in New York City. Although married multiple times, both were self-sufficient; they liked men, but they did not need them. Frances and Athalia were outspoken, educated and champions for the underdog. They loved animals and advocated on their behalf. They were community-minded. And although it was unusual for women to bear no children in those days, both Frances and Athalia were close to their nieces and made them their heirs.

It seemed that the oldest city could not bear such a strong strain of atypical women. It was an unsustainable environment, and Frances and Athalia were gone in the blink of an eye. It was almost as though something sought to eradicate them, to pick them off before their influence spread. Some formless, nameless nemesis was stalking the streets, and one street in particular, wreaking vengeance on the oldest city. It was enough to make a person feel that beneath the surface lay another path of desecrated history and ignoble deeds—of evil, rudely awakened, haunted and arisen, come home to roost.

One woman comes home from a shopping excursion and, minutes later, ends up dead, nearly decapitated on the front steps of her home in broad daylight on a busy street. Ten months later, another woman has her head bashed in during her nightly walk, and her body is set on fire in a deserted lot. In both cases, residential neighbors surrounded the doomed women. No one deserved such an ignoble end, particularly Frances Ashworth Bemis, who vigorously and fearlessly walked a mile or two every single night. Her death wasn't a robbery. She never carried a purse during her walks, only a flashlight. Although her clothes were torn and disheveled, she wasn't raped. The night she died, neighbors heard screams and the voice of a woman shrieking, "Oh, oh, oh." A Miss Virginia Wrigley said, "It sounded just like a child screaming. I opened the shade and said, 'What's the matter? What's the matter? What's the matter?' I called the police, but nobody came to do anything."

Police did, in fact, clock the call at 7:04 p.m. Officer Kenton checked the area. He wrote in his report, "Could not find anyone or anything around." He did not check with the neighbor who made the call. If the assailant was still roaming the streets, it escaped his attention.

Early in the morning on November 4, 1974, a Mrs. Davis of 11 Bridge Street made a grisly discovery while walking her dog. She called the police to report a corpse lying in a vacant lot just south of 46 Marine Street. Her dog led her directly to the body and tried to lie down next to it.

Officer Booth arrived around 7:42 a.m., took one look, called his supervisor and told him about the body, adding, "Her head is busted open and the brain is in clear view." There was dried blood on Frances's head. One eye was gouged, and her face was smashed. Almost every bone in her body was broken. Cloth from her own dress was wrapped tightly around her

Former vacant lot where Frances Bemis's body was found in 1974. *Photo by Bob Randall.*

neck, and her legs and one arm were singed. Someone had tried to burn the body. Naturally, there was no sign of life. Booth called an ambulance.

Eight minutes later, another officer, Hewitt, arrived, and the men secured the area. Someone called Assistant State Attorney Richard Watson, who personally inspected the crime scene. Everyone learned his lesson from the debacle that accompanied Athalia's death. There were no mistakes this time. Frances's nearly nude body was covered with a sheet, borrowed from a neighbor, but nothing was moved.

Someone called the FDLE, and it dispatched a unit from the Jacksonville lab. Local police maintained security of the area until the special agents arrived. Then, all of them, including Police Chief Virgil Stewart, assisted in collecting evidence. This included three pieces of cement block, ashes, the sheet used to cover Frances's body, a key, pearls, a flashlight, a button, fingerprints, a piece of denim cloth, hair, blood and the pieces of her torn and disheveled clothes. The body was so battered that it was unidentified for a week until dental records were made and compared. The medical examiner, Dr. Peter Lipkovic, wrote that she died of severe crushing head injuries. Her friend Nancy Powell and her lawyer, Charles Bennett, tentatively identified her mutilated body. But everyone knew that the murdered woman was Frances Bemis. She was always in touch, and no one had heard from her that week. Also, her porch light was still on, and Frances, careful with her dollars, never wasted electricity.

The city police and the county sheriff's office worked on this case together, just as they had with Athalia's murder, and with no better results. It was not for lack of effort. Officers, deputies and special agents swept the neighborhood, interviewing everyone. They made up a list of local mental patients and sex offenders and tracked them down—although Frances was partially unclothed, she was not raped. They interviewed recent assault victims and looked for men released from the state prison in Raiford. Sheriffs Virgil Stewart and Dudley Garrett followed every lead and contacted law enforcement in every state for similar crimes. Even the Federal Bureau of Investigation (FBI) became involved.

The brown Caucasian hairs found on Frances were not hers, and the button was not from her clothes, nor was the scrap of denim cloth. The FBI requested the fingerprints of Alan Stanford and of another man, Gerald Austin. Both men were listed as suspects in the official FBI report. Alan Stanford was a logical suspect, although he was never charged. Little is known about Gerald Austin. His name was not found on any of the police reports, only on the FBI report. There is no other information available about him except that a man of his name lived on Eugene Street in St. Augustine at that time, worked somewhere as a "manager" and was married to a woman named Ruth.

Sheriff Garrett offered a $500 reward on the front page of the *Record*, just as he did to gain evidence for Athalia's case. No one came forward. The police weren't buying the Alan Stanford theory. Alan was lying low, awaiting trial, and to kill a woman he barely knew on speculative evidence seemed unlikely. Also, the muster of rage apparent in Frances's death seemed personal, impulsive and opportunistic and not at all like an organized and a deliberate crime. No one could think of any reason why Frances would be targeted for such a heinous offense. True, she was outspoken, but Frances had a tender side as well. She loved children. She treasured handwritten notes from her great-niece, Sarah, whom she showered with gold beads, a locket and a jewel chest.

In the months before her death, she befriended a little boy named Clay Martin, who wrote a letter to the editor of the *Record* about his pet rooster named Lucifer. Always social, Frances threw a "rooster party" for Clay at her home. When the boy moved away shortly afterward, she helped him find a new home for Lucifer and kept in touch, writing the boy letters about his former pet and taking an interest in his studies and activities.

Like Athalia, she loved animals, and Frances objected fiercely to the cruel treatment of horses used for carriage excursions throughout the city. Her neighbors described her as "sometimes caustic," but that was just 1970s talk for a woman who fearlessly spoke her mind. Unlike Athalia, Frances was not a St. Johns County outsider by any means, although she was an unusual woman for her time. Brought up in Georgia, she was that rare combination—a southern intellectual with a social conscience. She left the South to forge her career in New York City as a publicist. Then she came back, bought an apartment house on Marine Street, renovated it and retired to St. Augustine in the late 1950s.

She was born on January 25, 1898, in Atlanta, Georgia, and as a young adult, she attended Oglethorpe University and the University of California. During the war, she enlisted in the Women's Auxiliary Army Corps and rose to the rank of corporal, organizing entertainment with the United Service Organization (USO). She was a good writer, but her social nature inclined her toward a career as a publicist. She went to New York City, reigning over marketing, using the social media of the mid-twentieth century to achieve spectacular success. She even organized an annual circus in Central Park around Thanksgiving every year—complete with clowns, elephants, bears, ponies, dogs and acrobats—when she worked for the publicity department at Hearn's department store. The newspaper coverage alone was worth thousands in advertising dollars. One colleague wrote to her in March 1950, "Dear Frances—Everyone is talking about you; about the way you manage everything; about the way you start things rolling; about your charm—I could go on and on…"

She ended up as the director of feature events for Abraham and Straus, a department store in New York City. From all accounts, Frances wore her power and prestige well. Her boss adored her. ("I'm running out of superlatives. Wonderful! Wonderful!") She worked like a Trojan and rarely took time off except to vacation in Florida. But the pace began to wear her down. In 1950, on her distinctive pink memo paper with a caricature of a lady wearing a hat and talking into a microphone, her name in stenciled print ("From Frances Bemis"), she wrote:

Maybe I won't come back to the mad-house. When I think of last night, and a fashion editor calling me at home to: "Darling, could you have your secretary send me out that darling little folding table I see advertised, and a half dozen vichyssoise." I could dream of a rowboat in the Everglades and hope never to return to editors who want folding tables in return for stories on milliners.

Meanwhile, the work went on. She organized fashion shows (Your Easter Silhouette) and promotions (Better Living with Television, Homemaker's Carnival). Pratt Institute wanted her to do a lecture series as part of its Professional Orientation Course. She spoke at the Women's Press Club and at an RKO banquet for the ambassador of Israel. Frances was a judge and a commentator for school and for city parades. She created newsreels for Fox Movie Time, which ran in thousands of theaters. On her pink notepaper, Frances wrote, "Keeping newspapers enthusiastic over giving us credits is a very important part of our work. We stay nights to photograph for National Magazines—from a Marten Towel color shot for Good Housekeeping to a table setting in color for Living."

The big city, the celebrities, the fast-paced life and the four marriages all took their toll. At the age of fifty-six, Frances chucked it all and moved to Marine Street in St. Augustine. Burning no bridges and always generous with praise, on June 5, 1956, she wrote to her employer, "When I leave I shall carry with me the feeling of pride, respect, and admiration I have always had for the president of the store [A&S] that has been my working 'home' for seven years."

In St. Augustine, however, Frances found it difficult to relax. The first thing she did was order new gold-embossed letterhead stationery featuring the city gates. Then she organized a welcoming committee for new residents and, in her typical fashion, made it a marketing success. Real estate firms sent her lists of new homeowners; she got Mayor Hahn involved and held meetings at his house. Within six months, she had expanded the program to twenty-five members. Frances, once again, was working like a Trojan, organizing, writing, getting the community involved and signing her correspondence on her new letterhead, "Yours, for a friendlier St. Augustine."

At some point in the spring of 1957, she seemed to realize that she was working just as hard as she did in New York City. She resigned from the welcoming committee, saying, "I shall not be able to carry on the work." If she hoped that her ideas for a kinder, gentler community would persevere without her leadership, she was wrong. By the time Athalia arrived in town, sixteen years later, the misanthropic attitude of the oldest city toward newcomers was still firmly and obviously embedded.

On her end, though, Frances never lacked for friends or for companionship. Anne Heymen, retired reporter at the *Record*, recalled Frances's house and some of the social events Frances hosted. It was a hard-drinking and a chain-smoking crowd in the '60s, and Frances, with her heavy lidded eyes, her cultured drawl and her vibrant curiosity, was right in the center of it all. However, she never succumbed to a life solely of fun and games, even in her retirement.

Frances was involved with local art galleries and was a member of each. She donated her furs to the St. Johns Mental Health Association. She contributed to the St. Johns County Citizens Advisory Council on Aging. The St. Augustine Humane Society was on her list of charities. She donated photos and papers to the St. Augustine Historic Society and Preservation Board. She donated a refrigerator to the local NAACP office and paid her dues to become a member. And it was not just a philanthropic donation. Frances was an active participant.

At a time when the white citizenry of St. Augustine viewed the struggle for equal rights as an "intrusion" from behind their locked doors, Frances Bemis wrote, "I was there. Marching and protesting. I was right at the scene of this horror—almost the only white person outside of the troublemakers—none of my friends would go to town or around the Plaza during the demonstrations."

During the civil rights turmoil of the 1960s in St. Augustine, Frances Bemis was one of the few white local citizens marching with integrationists, bravely bearing the violent brunt of what she called "the red-neck whites who created it all—plus our own sheriff [L.O. Davis]. The blacks, led by King, were decent, orderly, and never belligerent."

The passage of the Civil Rights Act in 1964 was not the end of it for Frances. She collected and presented clippings of black academic achievers to Bethune-Cookman College, which the faculty spotlighted in its library, calling it "The Frances Bemis Scrapbook." The president of the college, Dr. Richard Moore, wrote to her, "It is individuals like you who give us the inspiration and encouragement to continue our task of education."

Dr. Moore invited Frances to the sixty-eighth commencement exercises, which she attended after a personal tour of the campus and a visit to the former home of "beloved Mrs. Bethune." Frances liked to write letters, to exhort, uplift and encourage. On Thanksgiving Day 1973, less than a year before her brutal murder, she wrote to Dr. Moore, "On this lovely Thanksgiving Day, I want to express my thankfulness that Florida has Bethune-Cookman College and Dr. Moore as its dedicated able president. Someday I look forward to making a contribution, perhaps

Smith College Collection, where Frances Bemis's private papers are archived. *Photo by Bob Randall.*

a legacy." Frances had "a special idea" for a legacy that she wanted to discuss with Dr. Moore.

After Frances died, the executor of her will donated all of Frances's papers and photographs to the Sophia Smith Collection at Smith College in Northampton, Massachusetts, fourteen catalogued boxes in all. Surely, within those boxes, in Frances's personal papers, resided the answer to the question everyone still wanted to know: was Frances murdered because she was writing a book revealing the identity of Athalia's killer?

Within the archives of Frances's collection, there is evidence that she was writing a book, but it was not about Athalia. She wrote a ten-page book proposal ("A Woman Alone") in 1959, outlining the story of her marketing success in New York City. It could've been a good book. Any person interested in marketing would do well to study Frances's methods. She wrote, "Today in my quiet St. Augustine home the exciting world of people whose lives touched mine for 25 years still come to me across the pages of my newspapers, magazines, and books on TV and on radio. Al Capp, Vic Damone, Madame Alexander, Elizabeth Arden, author Betty Smith—I have known all of these celebrated people and hundreds more in my life in public relations."

Unfortunately, after a lifetime of writing press releases, Frances had a hard time putting together a cohesive book-length narrative. The manuscript was never completed. Frances also left behind several pages of notes, titled "Murder on Marine Street," but the notes were not for a book she was writing. They were suggestions for a book someone else was writing—probably her friend Nancy Powell. Her suggestions were good: "My feeling is you should start with the horror—building up to the Marine Street setting—people gardening, listening to early news, preparing dinner—then, wow—catapulted into the most sensational happening in the Oldest City's history. Describe all the horrendous details—THE WONDERMENT—who could possibly have done such a brutal killing? Was there a MANIAC LOOSE?"

Indeed, there was. More than one, apparently. However, Frances Bemis knew nothing about their identities. Also, in her papers, there was a letter from Sheriff Garrett, responding to a letter and a clipping she sent him about a spate of murders up north and her suggestion that they could be related to Athalia's demise. She was just guessing like everyone else.

Frances's murder is a cold case in St. Johns County, still unsolved to this day. According to Dominic Nicklo, the police never believed that Alan Stanford had anything to do with Frances's murder. However, they were convinced that he killed Athalia. Two months after Frances died, Alan's murder trial began.

THE TRIAL

St. Augustine is the most lawless city I've ever seen.
—Martin Luther King Jr.

There are no court records of the 1975 trial of *The State v. Alan Stanford Jr.* When asked about the location of the files, records officials in St. Johns County and in the sheriff's department speculate that perhaps the trial was never transcribed. But if it was, the records are gone. *Poof.*

Since official sources don't know what happened to the court transcripts, or even if court transcripts ever existed, the only available documented information concerning the murder trial that attempted to bring Athalia's alleged killer to justice is compiled within the microfilmed archives of the *St. Augustine Record* and the *Florida Times- Union.*

MONDAY, TUESDAY, WEDNESDAY, JANUARY 20–22, 1975

Monday, January 20, was a damp and overcast day. The headline on the front page of the *St. Augustine Record* blared, "Alan Stanford Trial—Jury Selection Begins." Under the brooding sky, the picture of a positively jaunty Alan Stanford—slight smile, shoulders squared—contrasted with the anguished expression on the face of his wife, Patti, whose hand he clasped "on the way to the courthouse." A retinue of defense attorneys, family and friends trailed them.

Manslaughter

Man H

One man is dead and another is charged with manslaughter in the aftermath of an altercation Sunday afternoon in northwestern St. Johns County, according to sheriff's deputies.

The dead man is Vernon Kruse, 48, who resided in a trailer village near Palmo Fish Camp and at 5515 Bishop Circle, Jacksonville, according to investigative reports filed in connection with the case.

CHARGED WITH manslaughter in Kruse' death is 40-year-old Raymond Hilgerson, who resides in a mobile home along State Road 13, just north of Joe Ashton Road, and in the same area of the county in which Kruse resided.

Hilgerson was arrested initially on a charge of murder in the first degree, according to Lt. Bob Bissell, who signed the arrest affidavit Sunday afternoon. However, the charge was reduced to manslaughter by the state attorney's office this morning.

THE ARREST affidavit alleges that Hilgerson killed Kruse by hitting him with a rifle.

On Way To Courthouse Alan G. Stanford Jr., former St. Johns County manager, clasps the hand of his wife, Patti, as they walk with defense attorneys to the county courthouse where his trial on a charge of murdering his neighbor, Mrs. Athalia Ponsell Lindsley, opened today.

Record Photo By DENNIS WINN

Alan Stanford Trial

Jury Selection Begins

By PAUL MITCHELL
Editor

jury duty in the long-awaited murder trial involving former County Manager

State Prosecutor Stephen Boyles of Daytona Beach, question prospective

The trial begins. *Courtesy of the St. Augustine Record.*

About 125 men and women were waiting in the courthouse. The air conditioner broke down. Judge Eastmoore tried to soothe the uncomfortable prospective jurors, saying that he expected to seat a jury by Wednesday and to conclude the whole trial within seven to ten days. Another 125 jurors were to show up the following day if a panel were not approved. The selection of the twelve jurors was crucial because the verdict of the jury had to be unanimous.

The prosecution representing the state was State Attorney Stephen Boyles and Assistant State Attorney Richard Watson. Boyles wasn't local, but Richard Watson was active in many civic affairs in St. Johns County. Representing Alan was Frank Upchurch Jr. and partners Edward Booth and Walter Arnold from Jacksonville. Frank Upchurch was a crucial factor in identifying St. Johns County residents who might be sympathetic to Alan's case and recommending them as jurors.

The first day of questioning by Judge Eastmoore and by State Attorney Boyles proved "that every single juror had knowledge from the news media of the brutal slaying of Mrs. Lindsley." Acquaintances and admitted supporters of Alan were supposedly dismissed. By Tuesday, January 21, the defense and the prosecution had approved eight jurors and were down to the last four. Frank Upchurch Jr. was quoted in the *Record*, "It's moving slower than we'd hoped, but with eight persons tentatively seated, we're hoping we can finish this phase soon."

A lawyer, observing the trial, remarked to a reporter that "the defense won't tolerate a juror with a solid auditing background. They want to add everything in life on a two plus two basis, and they get really upset if everything doesn't fit right." All prospective jurors professed their approval of capital punishment. They guaranteed no personal relationships with Alan or with the witnesses. Neither the state nor the defense used all its preemptory challenges that second day, challenges that enabled them to remove jurors without cause.

The state saved the rest of its challenges for the final day of jury selection. To no one's surprise, the defense never used all of its challenges, as it didn't need to. St. Augustine citizenry were overwhelmingly sympathetic to Alan Stanford. The *St. Augustine Record*, thanks to Patrick Lynn, was complicit in its support. Thankfully, another editor, Paul Mitchell, was covering the trial.

The lawyers finished jury selection in two and a half days. The panel was composed of seven men, five women and two alternates, a man and a woman. Three were black and nine were white. Judge Eastmoore denied the state's motion to move the trial to Volusia County because of the expedience of the jury selection and because no one admitted prejudice because of the media coverage. The jury was not sequestered, but Judge Eastmoore cautioned the jurors "to refuse to discuss the upcoming trial, or past events with anyone outside the courtroom." The *St. Augustine Record* printed the names and the addresses of the jurors on the front page of the newspaper on January 22, 1975.

Sheriff Garrett issued admission tickets, which allowed spectators into the small courtroom. Sally Boyles, wife of prosecutor Stephen Boyles, went every day. She said, "It was very intense. It was different from your ordinary trial—because of the level of violence. There was just an undertone of violence at that trial. It was such a horrible and vicious trial. It was full of undercurrents of pressure on every one."

THURSDAY, JANUARY 23, 1975

One year to the day after Athalia's brutal murder, the *St. Augustine Record* printed the headline "Jury Hears Grisly Murder Details" alongside a picture of Athalia looking gaunt and grim and wearing pearls. Jurors looked at other pictures of Athalia. They observed black-and-white pictures of what she looked like after she was hacked to death on the front steps of her home at 124 Marine Street. Alan Stanford watched their faces as they looked. Only one juror betrayed any emotion.

Defense attorneys Walter Arnold and Edward Booth objected to the state introducing the death scene photos. Booth said the photos were "so vile that they only serve one purpose—to inflame the minds of the jury." They were overruled by Judge Eastmoore. "They may be gruesome," he said, "but it's not up to the defendant to determine." He said the pictures were necessary to establish position and premeditation.

The three opening witnesses in the trial were James Rosseau, the ambulance attendant who hosed down the murder scene; St. Augustine police sergeant Ronald Janson; and Dr. Arthur Schwartz, the medical examiner. Rosseau said that he was there within minutes after the emergency call from the sheriff's dispatcher. He said Athalia's body was still warm when he got there. Sergeant Janson said he and another officer were eating dinner on Anastasia Island when they got the call on their patrol car radios and returned to duty. He recalled seeing the covered corpse outside 124 Marine Street. He said he "tried" to secure the crime scene. Walter pressed the point that no fingerprints were taken.

State Calls Three Witnesses

Jury Hears Grisly Murder Details

St. Augustine R
Thursday
January

Mrs. Athalia Ponsell Lindsley   Defense attorneys Edward Booth and Walter Arnold of Jacksonville objected   The pathologist said Mrs. Lindsley

First day of testimony. *Courtesy of the St. Augustine Record.*

Dr. Schwartz said that the cause of Athalia's death was "almost complete decapitation." He said the dead woman "[s]uffered a mutilated right elbow from a sharp cutting blow that severed two and a half inches of bone and almost cut away the upper arm. The right wrist was almost in the same condition, with the right hand only dangling by tissue." Two fingers were also severed.

Dr. Schwartz continued, "One single clean blow from the back of the head, down through the skull and neck bone, and through a main artery was the main cause of death." He said it would take a powerful person standing fairly close to Athalia to have delivered such mutilation. He said the weapon used to inflict the damage was a machete. It was a good day for the prosecution.

FRIDAY, JANUARY 24, 1975

This was the day Locke McCormick, the state's only eyewitness, took the stand. Locke stuck with the story that he told Patricia Stanford the night of the murder: he didn't know. The *St. Augustine Record* bore the headline, "State Witness Seems Vague." Jacksonville's *Florida Times-Union* paper was headlined "Lindsley Case Eyewitnessed?" and "Witness Not Sure of Man's Identity."

Locke's grandmother Mrs. Claude Smith testified, "I was in the kitchen with my daughter. Previously, we heard noises. Hacking sounds. Muffled moans." Mrs. Smith and Mrs. McCormick went into the den, but Locke wasn't there. Then he rushed into the house around 6:00 p.m. asking for the telephone numbers of the police and an ambulance. "I've never seen him so upset," she testified.

She heard Locke say, "Mr. Stanford is hitting Mrs. Ponsell." This exclamation was kept out of the papers and was not widely known. Then Locke called an ambulance to the scene. The jury was dismissed, and Walter argued that the testimony was hearsay and inadmissible. Richard Watson disagreed. Judge Eastmoore said that he'd studied the problem and found it admissible as a "bystander's spontaneous statement."

Richard Watson asked Mrs. Smith if she recalled telling him that Alan came to her house three days after the murder and told her that he saw Athalia in her yard on the afternoon of the day she died. He and Mrs. Smith had a laugh over the fact that Athalia was "wearing something other than a pink robe," which Athalia apparently wore when gardening. Of course,

Athalia was not in her yard that day, despite what Alan said. She was in Jacksonville with her husband.

Then Locke, wearing a brown a suit, took the stand. He said that he saw a man with graying hair wearing a white dress shirt and dark dress trousers—a man he first thought was Stanford—walking away from the Lindsley home seconds after Athalia's death. He spoke of his view of the partially obscured right shoulder of a man in a white dress shirt with the sleeves rolled up standing on Athalia's front steps and, a few seconds later, seeing a man with gray-streaked hair walking toward the Stanford home. He spoke of seeing Athalia lying on the front steps of her home with the eyes of her nearly severed head turned toward him. As Richard and Stephen cross-examined him, however, Locke grew more and more vague. He said that his mother, Rosemary, asked him if he was sure it was Stanford, and at the time, he felt it was. Now, he was not sure. In fact, Locke felt it could not have been Stanford. "It was nobody I'd ever seen before," he said. Locke did not budge from his testimony.

Two reporters, Nancy Powell of the *Times-Union* and Jackie Feagin of the *St. Augustine Record*, testified that day. Nancy was a friend of Athalia's, and Jackie was a friend of the Stanfords. Nancy Powell testified that Alan, a fellow member of Trinity Episcopal congregation, called her on a Wednesday after a commission meeting. "He called to ask if I knew any dirt on Mrs. Lindsley," she said. "He wanted to know if I knew anything bad about her." Alan wanted to know how many times Athalia had been married. Nancy said that Alan told her, "If she doesn't stop doing what she's doing, I'm going to send her back where she came from." Nancy said she asked him if he meant Jacksonville, and Alan said, "No. Where she came from."

Jackie Feagin spoke about covering county commission meetings for the newspaper and seeing Athalia "criticize" Stanford in 1973 on October 9 and November 13, 1973, and January 22, 1974. She testified that at the October 9 session, "Mrs. Lindsley said, 'He threatened my life.'" Jackie said that Alan attempted to deny it, but "he was prevented from making any further statement by the county commission chairman [Herbie Wiles]."

Emrich and Murphy, the two Florida State Board of Professional Engineers officials, testified that day for the state. They said that Alan admitted he signed papers as county engineer, although he was only the city manager. "We planned to interview Mrs. Lindsley the next day," Emrich said. Not a good day for the state or for the defense.

SATURDAY, JANUARY 25, 1975

The headline on the front page of the *St. Augustine Record* read, "Key Question: Where Was Stanford? And What Was He Wearing?"

Young Patricia Stanford was called to the stand by the state, perhaps in desperation after Locke's disastrous testimony. When Richard Watson presented the many inconsistencies of her initial testimony to the court, Patricia, described as a "comely brunette," said, "It was early in the morning. I was sleepy. That morning last February I was giving impulse answers." Among the many "impulse answers" that were in conflict with her original testimony were what her father was wearing and what time he got home, what time she and her mother got home, which door her mother exited from when she heard screams and so on. She said that Alan was there when she got home, wearing paint-splattered clothing, and "there was no time in all of that excitement to tell the time of day."

Stephen Boyles said, "Yes, but there was time to swing." Boyles was pointing out that after looking out her bedroom window at Athalia's blood-soaked body, Patricia took three-year-old Annette outside to swing on the playset.

Patricia said, "Yes, but when you have a little baby, you can't get them upset." This was the second time in recorded testimony that Patricia Stanford referred to Annette Stanford as "her" baby. Despite her obvious affection for and her closeness to the child, she did not think twice about taking her out of an unlocked door and into the backyard, next door to a neighbor who had just been brutally hacked to death. If the state questioned Patricia about that incongruence, it was not mentioned in the newspapers.

Boyles did ask her if she noticed Alan's shoes or his belt when he finally got home that night. If Alan murdered Athalia, he could not have been wearing either because he would have chucked them in the San Sebastian River at the end of Riberia Street prior to returning home.

"I didn't notice," Patricia said. She did notice that he returned with an engineering book and a slide rule, two items that Alan said he returned to the office to get. She said she had no clue of the feud between Athalia and her father until she read about it in the papers. But on February 1, 1974, she said to Richard Watson, "The woman [Mrs. Lindsley] caused him so much trouble I figured if they couldn't find him [the murderer] that they might point the finger at him."

A year later, on the stand, she said, "From reading the papers I learned how horrible the murder was, and I wondered if they found who did it." She blinked her eyes hard as she delivered this statement.

Patricia's friend, Student of the Month Hunter Barnett, testified next, saying that Patti Stanford dropped her off at home at about 5:45 p.m. instead of about 5:10 p.m., as Patricia and her mother claimed. Hunter's stepfather, Jesse Miller, confirmed Hunter's estimate, calculating it approximately from when he heard the sound of the cannon fired at 5:00 p.m. from the Guard Arsenal, as it was every day.

Arnold asked, "Could the cannon have been fired from the Castillo de San Marcos fort and not been the Guard's 5 p.m. signal?" Miller said no. But the jury heard the question.

Patrolman Francis O'Loughlin, one of the initial investigating officers on the scene, said that he examined Athalia's body and searched the two-story house. Except for the dog, either Chico or Zsa Zsa, from which no one heard a peep, the house was unoccupied. Then he saw Stanford pull up "from the south of Charlotte Street at 6:55 p.m. and park in the back yard near the fence separating the two houses. 'Stanford said he had just returned from his office to pick up some books and he had a book and slide rule in his hands,'" O'Loughlin said.

O'Loughlin "advised him that there had been a homicide next door. Stanford asked if she had been shot or cut," O'Loughlin recalled. After the officer observed the "trail of blood" from the murder scene leading to "about the center of the wall separating the two houses," O'Loughlin interviewed Alan two more times. Stanford commented that he and Athalia "had not been the best of friends."

Walter hammered O'Loughlin to admit that the blood trail led to the southwest corner of Charlotte Street. What he did not say was that it stopped at Alan's car. He did say that the blood could have been tracked by the police or by other people intruding the crime scene. He pointed out that the bottom of the screen on Athalia's kitchen door was torn. What he did not say was that it was probably a convenient way for her to let the dogs in and out.

Then the wrangling about the machete began. Freddie Hudnall, survey crew supervisor, was not put on the stand, but two crew members, David Wehking and Ricardo Edralin, confirmed that Alan had borrowed the machete in December and said that he returned it, although there was no record of that ever occurring.

Walter made sure the jury heard that the survey truck was usually unlocked during the day and that Alan could have put the machete back himself. But then what happened to it? Walter made the point, his first try at throwing an evidence witness under the bus, that Dewey Lee, who worked in the county garage (and who found the murder weapon and Alan's clothes in the city dump), was the one who usually serviced the county truck—where the machetes were stored. And he managed, somehow, to identify the machete that Alan borrowed and returned—without telling anyone he was returning it—and stole it for his own purposes.

It should have been a cautiously optimistic day for the state. But Walter had planted seeds of doubt that he intended to sow when the defense presented its case.

MONDAY, JANUARY 27, 1975

The headline on the front page of the *St. Augustine Record* read, "Defense Questions Lindsley About Machete."

In his book *Not Guilty*, Walter characterized the info about Alan borrowing the machete and never returning it as a "leak" to the media. Whether or not that was true, it was a fact that Florida "landscaping" in the '70s usually amounted to the man of the house swinging a machete at some palm fronds and spiny underbrush. Owning a machete was not the issue; everyone owned one. The question was which machete was used to murder Athalia Ponsell Lindsley? Was it the one Dewey Lee pulled out of the marsh near the city dump? Or was it the machete James Lindsley, the widower, carried around in the trunk of his car to hack at undergrowth in the houses he showed to prospective real estate clients?

The police had already wrestled with this issue, but there it was again. And why the defense was introducing evidence during the state's case was a mystery. But Walter came up with an eighteen-inch machete about which a mystified James Lindsley, upon examining it, could only say, "All machetes look alike to me."

Walter wasn't through. While Alan Stanford watched closely from the defendant's seat, Walter set out to eviscerate James. The jury heard that Athalia wrote to her sister, Geraldine, that James was "a thief and a liar." They heard that Athalia changed the locks on her house and didn't give James the key. They heard how James stole fifty dollars from an envelope she asked him to mail to a radio evangelist, resulting in a celebrated fight. Yet all James said in his defense was, "I thought it was a whimsical thing to do."

If objections were raised to this line of questioning, it didn't make the newspapers. Walter even said that he'd produce a witness to dispute James's testimony about his whereabouts on the day of his wife's murder, but Eastmoore finally stopped him and said, "I'll hear your witness at the proper time." The witness was never produced.

Why Richard Watson and Stephen Boyles allowed this during the presentation of their case is a mystery. Perhaps they were in shock. Perhaps they felt so confident that they thought it didn't matter. Why Walter pursued this line of questioning was no mystery at all. All he needed to establish in the minds of an already sympathetic jury was reasonable doubt. There was no evidence of blood on the machete that James willingly took out of the back seat of his car and turned over to Sheriff Garrett. As to the quarreling, all newlyweds squabble, and there were many instances of mutual affection between James and Athalia, especially on the day she died.

Walter even opened the old wound of Lillian Lindsley's death in a car crash on New Year's Eve in Duval County three years ago, with James at the wheel. "Didn't your first wife die a violent death?" he asked. He made sure the jury knew that James contested Athalia's will and forced Geraldine to settle on the 124 Marine Street house, splitting the proceeds of the sale. "I told my wife I made a new will and left half my estate to my son, and one half to her," Lindsley protested to the jury. But the damage was done.

TUESDAY, JANUARY 28, 1975

The front page of the *Florida Times-Union* read, "Bloody Evidence Entered in Stanford Trial." The front page of the *St. Augustine Record* noted, "State Introduces Machete in Murder Trial—Defense Tries to Implicate Finder."

Late Tuesday afternoon, the bloody evidence from the swamp was entered as evidence. Again, the defense tried throwing suspicion on Dewey Lee, who was the finder of this most compelling proof against Alan: bloody clothes, belt, shoes, wristwatch, paint- and blood-smeared diaper, human hair and the murder weapon. Walter Arnold was just doing what defense lawyers do, and in Dewey Lee, he found a foil to Alan. Where Alan was thin, educated and businesslike, with "a fine southern drawl," Dewey, six years older, was heavy, tired and a skilled laborer. He drank a lot, and he looked it. Where Alan could look cameras straight on and proclaim his innocence, Dewey looked down, mumbled, shifted and fidgeted in his seat. And with good reason. Almost as soon as he took the stand, Ed Booth "immediately began hammering at Lee… with questions inferring possible involvement in Mrs. Lindsley's death."

It was ludicrous of course. Dewey Lee didn't even know Athalia, and he would be no one's choice of a hit man—too slow. It was well established that he was at work during the time of the murder; there was a verified record and eyewitnesses. But Walter and Ed hinted about an eyewitness, Adelle McLoughlin, who, as she rode her bicycle down Marine Street on January 23, 1974, the day of the murder, claimed to have seen a "heavy-set white man in his late 50s opening the gate to the driveway" of Athalia's house about 4:30 p.m. Later, she was put on the stand and pointed to Dewey Lee as the man she saw that day. Adelle was the sister-in-law of Floyd Hardin, the county worker whom Alan allowed to stay in the lighthouse free of charge. (It was Floyd Hardin who swore that he saw Alan's car at the county office on the day and the time of the murder, although other, more reliable witnesses disputed his testimony. He admitted quite frankly that he wanted to "help" Alan.)

From the *St. Augustine Record*, "Booth asked Lee how he knew to look in the marshy area for evidence. Lee said, he figured the remote area would be a likely place to search." Booth pointed out that Dewey had graying hair like the man whose back Locke had seen chopping away at Athalia. While Dewey probably never wore a white dress shirt in his working life—not practical for a man who did oil changes under cars—Ed Booth made sure everyone knew that Dewey Lee handled machetes in his war days, saying, "Yes sir, I had 'em handy."

Ed Booth flustered Dewey so much that the man questioned whether the shoes he saw in court were the same as those found at the marsh. Alan's lawyers made sure that the jurors knew that the shoes entered as evidence were an eighth-inch bigger than the size Alan normally wore: a 10C as opposed to a 9½D.

The trial was disrupted with worries about the jurors, one of whom came down with the flu. Walter threatened a mistrial. An alternate stepped up, and the *St. Augustine Record* promptly printed the alternate's name, profession (a Spuds potato and cabbage farmer) and the vicinity of where he lived.

The trial stretched on into the night when the state introduced the laundry owner, the jeweler and the tailor, all of whom swore that the items in the swamp belonged to Alan. The jeweler, Charles Tanner, had a repair receipt for the watch with matching identification numbers. The laundress, Jean Maltby, had an invisible ink identification, which showed up matching the shirt to Alan. The tailor, Kenneth Beeson Jr., had a credit card receipt for the shirt and pants. They had no reason to lie.

Incredibly, Walter and Ed protested that the evidence from the marsh "has not been linked to the defendant and may have been tampered with." Judge

Eastmoore replied, "With no evidence to the contrary it must be assumed police officials wouldn't tamper with evidence in their custody."

Walter felt this was a "gross error" on the part of Judge Eastmoore showing "a lack of continuity of evidence." Later, Walter and Patti Stanford would claim that the watch and the shirts were stolen from the house during the police search and planted for Dewey Lee to find. Walter quoted Osborn's *Proof of Handwriting* to discredit Patti's credit card signature. He said the distinctive dark trousers with the thin red stripe that Beeson remembered selling to Patti Stanford were of the same quality and design sold to many other customers.

It was a smoke screen that anyone should have seen through and that the state should have been able to discredit. But it remained to be seen what the jury thought of it—whether Walter's efforts stank of brimstone or whether his words were rays of light and truth. Could the police have tried to frame Alan? Did James Lindsley pay Dewey Lee to murder Athalia? The eyes of the jury told the story. It should not have been a good day for the defense, but it was.

WEDNESDAY, JANUARY 29, 1975

The front page of the *St. Augustine Record* read, "Blood Near Scene Same as Victim's?"

The courtroom was packed, although the testimony of "a young woman" lab technician, Janet Estes (characterized as a "pert brunette with shoulder-length hair"), was, really, the most boring and disheartening event of the trial.

The iron railing removed from Athalia's front steps because it had been hacked with her assailant's machete bore dents and scratches that did not match the rusty machete Dewey Lee found because of the deterioration of the weapon. The blood in Alan's car was not the same blood type as Athalia's—it belonged instead to a woman who fell off her bike and broke her arm near Alan's house two years before. Alan took her to the hospital, she bled on the seats and, apparently, Alan had not cleaned the county car in all that time.

The clothes, shoes, wristwatch, diaper and machete fished from the swamp did contain type A blood, which was Athalia's blood type. But the blood was compromised and so deteriorated by water that Estes could not tell if it was human or animal blood. She did say that no blood was found inside Athalia's house, aside from the bloody footprint left by the police.

Hair taken from the machete was "consistent with" Athalia's hair. But Ed Booth established that "there are minor differences and some similarities in hairs taken from different places of the head of any given individual."

Cross-examined by Ed Booth, Estes's testimony came across as insubstantial. Ed thundered that no blood tests were made on James Lindsley's car or on Dewey Lee's car. He pointed out that Estes had never seen the machete from James Lindsley's car either, let alone run any tests on it.

There was a fingerprint expert present, Edward Stafford, but no fingerprints were taken at the crime scene, and the defense made sure the jury knew that. Walter's point was that the state's case against Alan was purely circumstantial, and he said so to the jury. Walter again asked for a "directed verdict" of acquittal for Alan, saying the state had not proved its case. Judge Eastmoore denied his motion. State Attorney Stephen Boyles shot back that he thought the evidence alone "was sufficient to identify the assailant" and challenged Walter by saying, "It doesn't seem to me that Mr. Arnold and I have been sitting through the same trial...but if there is to be a directed verdict at this time, it should be for the state."

At this point in the trial, Lieutenant Eddie Lightsey's absence as a witness for the state was painfully obvious. He was the one Dewey Lee called to report the blood-soaked evidence at the dump. He was the one who'd tagged it and turned it in. He was the lead investigator. Where was he? Ed Booth even went so far as to say, "What did Mr. Lightsey...put in his pocket during the search of Stanford's home that he didn't tell the sheriff about?"

Obviously, the state thought Eddie Lightsey would not help its case. Why? Because he had a grudge against Alan for firing his son? Whatever the reason, it was odd, and it lent credence to Walter's claim that the police planted evidence. There are people in St. Augustine today who believe that story, just as there are people who believe that Mark Foreman planted that glove in O.J. Simpson's yard the night Nicole Simpson and Ronald Goldman were hacked to death by an unknown assailant.

The state rested its case.

Thursday, January 30, 1975

The front page of the *St. Augustine Record* read, "Defense: Other Suspects, Leads Ignored—State 'Out to Get' Stanford."

Ed Booth did most of the cross-examining while the state presented its case. Walter Arnold took over during the presentation of the defense's case. He started by saying, "He [Alan Stanford] was at his office when this thing [murder] occurred next door to his home." Walter was focused on the jury. He was a good lawyer, and over the years, he cannily learned the strategies he needed to use in order to win cases. First and foremost, he immersed himself. That was the reason he only took cases "that interested him." He wanted something to engross his attention, and he became the expert concerning everything that had to do with case. He was sharp and alert. Nothing escaped his attention.

He sounded amazingly plausible—if you wanted to believe that Alan Stanford was innocent, if you didn't want to look too closely and if you didn't want "the unpleasantness" of having to deal with a public official who enacted the basest of human instincts. People had socialized with the Stanfords, and they had the Stanfords over to go out on the boat. Of course he wasn't guilty. It was all nonsense. A man would have to be crazy to do something like that. Alan was as typical a member of St. Augustine society as it was possible to get in the oldest city.

Walter made sure everyone remembered that Alan was from Atlanta, and so was Patti—two true-blue southern Americans. Their parents were well connected, and Alan went to Clemson and Emery. He served in the merchant marines. He worked for Fairchild and then for the county. He was a father.

That whole thing about Athalia reporting him for illegally signing city documents as the county engineer? That was no big deal. "Alan," Walter said, "did not even use that title." Walter sounded so reasonable; it was almost a relief to the jury and spectators to hear his words. "The county commission knew when they hired him that he was a marine engineer."

Walter went on. Alan did most of the "rebuilding and renovations" of the house on Marine Street. Everyone in the neighborhood got along well until Athalia moved in and "began accumulating dogs and goats." The dynamics of the neighborhood feud were explained away as, "Alan had nothing to do with the complaints and he did not appear at the trials."

But for some inexplicable reason, Athalia "turned her wrath" against Alan. Walter portrayed Athalia as mentally unstable after she criticized the county commissioners for spending a lot of money on the salary of a public official who wasn't really qualified to do the job. But, Walter said, "this thing did not get under his hide…he didn't smolder, and he had no motive whatsoever to kill Mrs. Lindsley." As soon as Walter said that, it was clear to the astute observer that Walter was going to put Alan on the stand. He had to. The jury had to hear it out of Alan's own mouth. They had to hear him say, "I did not kill Athalia Ponsell Lindsley." They wanted to believe him. But they had to watch his face and his eyes when he said it.

On the other hand, it must have crossed the jurors' minds that if Alan *wasn't* guilty, then someone else *was*. And who could it be? At that point, there was nowhere else to turn. If you looked at the facts, there was no other plausible suspect. Period. No one seriously believed that James, the former mayor, or Dewey Lee, the humble mechanic, had anything to do with it. At that point, even though momentum for Alan's acquittal continued to accumulate, people began to face facts. They rooted for Alan, but they knew the truth even if they did not want to look it in the eye.

And Walter made it so easy. It would be easy to think, "Yes, it was the way he said it was." Whether you truly believed it or not. Depending on Alan's testimony.

Friday, January 31, 1975

"Stanford Takes Stand in His Own Defense," read the headline of the *St. Augustine Record*. "Stanford Grilled Over His Alibi" blared the bold typeface on the *Florida Times-Union*, which also added, "No Motive to Murder, Stanford Insists."

Dixon, Fox and Hardin all testified that Alan's car was at the county office at the time when the murder occurred. Richard Watson did a pretty good job of picking apart their inconsistent testimony. Dixon was a criminal. Fox couldn't remember if he had the right date, and he'd been drinking. Hardin owed Stanford because he lived in the county lighthouse. Patti Stanford testified and was characterized as "incoherent" on the stand.

Then Alan Stanford testified. Sally Boyles said his was the most compelling testimony during the trial. Walter also said it was good, but he was disappointed in Alan's "lack of warmth." Alan testified that he had "no motive" to kill Athalia and "I had no feud with anyone." He did say, "I thought she might have some criminal background." Also, the menagerie that Athalia kept had grown since previous testimony. Alan established that it included two goats and numerous dogs. But he took all of this "in a light vein."

Walter got Alan to say that neither he nor his wife was home during the sheriff's search of his house, and afterward their home "was a scene of devastation." The testimony was risky. Walter was worried that the state would see it as an open door to introduce the actual evidence police seized during the search. He feared this, which was why he'd suppressed the evidence in the first place. It would be hard to stand down a police officer, to look him in the eye in front of the jury, and accuse him of lying when he said, "I did not take Mr. Stanford's watch. Or shirt, or shoes or pants." Then there was the matter of the bloody concrete block, which was part of the evidence the police took from Alan's shed. But showing Alan as a victim of the police was crucial, and Walter's fears were unfounded. Stephen Boyles, eager to get on with Alan Stanford in cross-examination, let the opportunity slide.

Stephen Boyles asked Alan, "Would you describe the difficulty with Mrs. Lindsley…as a nightmare or as a feud?"

Alan, "immaculate in a grey suit and a dark tie," answered, "I do not describe it as either."

"How would you describe it?"

"You just described it for me—as a difficulty." He wasn't angry with Athalia, Alan explained. He thought, "She was mentally deranged."

Alan's demeanor was described in the papers as demonstrating "coolness, concentration and memory of testimony and evidence introduced during the 12-day trial." This trial was the test that Alan was truly studying for, and he dare not fail it as he'd failed his engineering exam. Walter Arnold wasn't the only person there immersed in the trial. Alan's life was at stake. Judge Eastmoore was authorizing plea bargains: first life and then thirty years for a guilty plea. It would save his life. But Alan said no and redoubled his efforts to appear convincing on the stand. He *was* convincing.

Alan said, "I believed that if Mrs. Lindsley had been in a mental institution, this would show cause for her erratic actions…I thought hers was an unstable life and that the number of husbands might be useful."

"How would this be useful?"

"It would indicate an alien kind of attitude, and I understood she had five husbands." Alan described Athalia as "less than pleasant," but he "also recalled that many people who observed her actions in public considered her a 'nut.'"

Alan denied that he, his wife and his daughter synchronized their times as an alibi. "Certainly not," Alan said self-righteously. Stephen showed Alan the wristwatch entered as evidence, and Alan said, "I cannot say if it's mine." Alan repeated his statement that he'd returned the county machete to the van before the murder, but "Hudnall can't remember the incident."

Then Alan said the words everyone had waited to hear. He talked about how one of his employees asked him if he'd "killed Mrs. Lindsley." Alan paused, looked at the jury and said, "I told him, I did not." Anyone who has attended a murder trial has seen suspects just as good as Alan on the stand, and they were still convicted on less evidence. A lot less. It remained to be seen what the jury would do.

MONDAY, FEBRUARY 3, 1975

The front page of the *St. Augustine Record* read, "Verdict May Come Tonight—Stanford Trial in Midst of Summations."

It was the thirteenth day of the trial—an inauspicious omen, but for whom? Stephen Boyles spent two hours on his summation:

> *Evidence shows...that Stanford was simmering and smoldering when he came home after talks with two state engineering investigators that afternoon. The defendant had a couple of drinks...and he sat and read the paper. He got into a rage and took several drinks to bolster his courage and to release his inhibitions. Then he walked into the utility room, picked up a machete and walked outside and up to Mrs. Lindsley, and literally hacked that woman to death on that doorstep.*
>
> *Then he walked over the driveway with the machete dripping blood, with his wife at their back door and with Rosemary McCormick calling. He told his wife to go and keep Rosemary busy. Then, he went into the utility shed where he removed his belt and changed clothes, wiped with a towel and rolled the clothing together and put them in the back of his car. He drove to Riberia Street and got rid of the clothing, machete, and watch.*

Stephen scoffed at "ghosts" conjured up by the defense to explain the events of that deadly day. Dewey Lee's county work records showed him working in the bridge area north of the city that day. He said the idea that James Lindsley and the police tried to "frame" Stanford "is an exercise in fantasy and imagination. And there wasn't enough money involved for anybody to kill, and it couldn't have been a hit man. It's not hit-man style to kill on a busy street in broad daylight. You don't kill for profit with a machete. Lindsley had 1,000 better opportunities to do it, and the suggestion is totally ridiculous."

Stephen reminded jurors that Rosemary McCormick ran to the gate at the Lindsley front yard and saw Athalia lying on the front steps. Then she saw Patti come out of her house on her side of the fence, not out of the front door, as she'd testified. Rosemary asked her, "Where's Alan?" and Patti said, "I don't know."

Stephen said, "Mrs. Stanford's testimony that she thought a maniac was loose that afternoon…had she not seen her husband that day with the machete, she would not have stayed outside talking to Rosemary McCormick after viewing the victim lying in a pool of blood. She would have fled inside to protect her family and would have called her husband at his office to come home."

Stephen paused. "Athalia Ponsell Lindsley had the right to live no matter how much she antagonized Stanford. She was a strong-willed woman exercising her right to free speech when she attacked his credentials. Nobody deserved what she got."

Perhaps "deserved" was an unfortunate choice of words, because many people in St. Augustine openly and vocally opined that Athalia got exactly what she "deserved." How dare she criticize highly placed white men in her society? She was an obstacle, a problem, and one that had to be stopped—even if Alan *didn't* kill her. It was not a stretch to speculate that she antagonized some other man, the real killer. It was not a stretch to believe that her death was not only deserved but also, considering her scandalous behavior, inevitable.

Walter Arnold capitalized on the doubts lingering in the minds of the jurors during his summation. "Other persons, including Lindsley, could have had a motive for the murder," he said. Or "she was attacked by a maniac or she was attacked by a hired killer, someone not known in the neighborhood." Walter said the keys found in the back door suggested that the killer was in the house when Athalia got home that afternoon. Her estate could have been the motive for the crime. He speculated that thieves took Alan's clothing from the shed in the garage and tried to frame him. The state never looked at other suspects. And so on.

"They were after Stanford," Walter said firmly, casting Alan as the victim at Athalia's murder trial. He said that the articles found in the swamp were "removed from Alan's house during the police search, doctored by deputies, then given to Lee to place in the swamp and then recover." He shouted and he pounded the podium for emphasis.

Judge Eastmoore sequestered the jury over the weekend and up until Monday. The lawyers finished up around 6:00 p.m. By 8:35 p.m., the verdict was in.

TUESDAY, FEBRUARY 4, 1975

The front page of the *Florida Times-Union* read, "Jury Acquits Stanford of Murder." The front page of the *St. Augustine Record* blew up its font: "Stanford Is Acquitted."

Judge Eastmoore instructed the jurists, "In a case where circumstantial evidence is involved, a well-connected chain of circumstances should be considered as conclusive as positive evidence concerning guilt." During juror deliberations, the bailiffs brought in supper. In two hours, the jurors were back, filing into their seats. The courtroom was packed. Alan and his lawyers had to rise. As Walter Arnold famously titled his autobiographical book, the verdict was: Not Guilty.

Alan immediately and dramatically fell to his knees. Then he stood and thanked the jury. He rushed over to Patti and hugged and kissed her. Philip Whitley snapped a picture for the cover of the *Florida Times-Union* of the pair smiling and staring into each other's eyes. Then Alan embraced Patricia and Sherry. There is a picture in the *St. Augustine Record* captioned, "Stanfords All Smiles." It looks like a lineup at a holiday party, everyone close together, arms linked, beaming and looking at the camera, except for Patti, who is smiling but looks off into the distance.

Alan was quoted as saying he felt, "Great, just great." Then he added:

Thank God that the jury came to the verdict they did. It was no surprise, and I knew the truth would come out. Following my arrest, I requested of the County Commission that I be placed on leave of absence and I hope to resume my position as county manager, although I haven't discussed the possibility with any county officials as yet. We have a lot of pieces to pick up. My financial situation is just about devastated. And now I'll have to start building it up again.

He said nothing about paying back his father-in-law or the parishioners at Trinity Episcopal who passed the collection plate numerous times on his behalf.

The chairman of the county commission, Robert Curtan, was quoted in the same article: "Now that the results are in, if Stanford asks for his job back, we'll have to call a meeting in the near future and decide what to do about it. There is no way of predicting at this time what would be done."

But Fred Green, the county commissioner who prompted investigations of purchasing procedures and mass layoffs during Alan's two-year tenure, said only, "There is no chance that Stanford will be rehired as county manager." Significantly, there was no quote from Alan's good friend, Commissioner Herbie Wiles.

Oblivious to these developments, Alan prattled on happily to the press: "The evidence and testimony in the trial indicate some sort of plot and I was the scapegoat. I've been confident all along. As a matter of fact I prepared a statement of victory." *Victory* was an interesting word to use. It implied some kind of competition decided in his favor rather than a vindication, which would imply innocence.

A sidebar in the *St. Augustine Record* titled, "Good Family, God Made Life Bearable," expounded on Alan's views about his yearlong tenure as a martyr: "How does a human being survive more than a year of suspicion, accusation, investigation and 13 days of trial for murder? Alan G. Stanford,

The Stanford family all smiles after the verdict. *Courtesy of the St. Augustine Record.*

Jr. recalls his hell on earth…when asked 'how does a human being stand such pressures?' Alan replied, 'I can tell you. Yes, it has been rough, but I wish you would tell people that if a man has faith in God, and confidence in himself, and has a good family, he can make it.'"

Not everyone was so cheery. "Richard Watson said that the defense strategy of throwing suspicion on witnesses 'deters people from coming forward with knowledge of crimes. The defense doesn't accord Lee, Lindsley and Lightsey the same presumption of innocence accorded the defendant who's charged.'"

Sheriff Garrett announced his intention to close the case. "To continue would be to prosecute an innocent person," he said.

Stephen Boyles said, "We are tired and glad it's over."

Walter Arnold recalled the joy the acquittal brought to his daughter, Terri, an airline stewardess who lived in Atlanta. Terri took vacation time to help her father with the trial, mostly in the form of fetching snacks, giving encouragement and befriending the Stanfords. She hugged and kissed every one of them and told her father, "See, Dad? I knew we'd win."

Walter spoke on behalf of his law firm: "We had confidence in our case and we had confidence in our client and justice has prevailed again." Walter wasn't wrong. Justice in 1975 in St. Augustine did prevail. But what did it look like forty years later?

Epilogue

2015

No one ever really gets away with anything.
Sometimes we're just not around for the end.
—anonymous

You do your job, you live your life, and wherever you end up is where you end up.
—Dominic Nicklo

At the end of the trial, everyone picked up the pieces and went home. In spite of what Alan said, the conclusion of the trial was a "victory" for no one. Athalia was still dead. Alan, in spite of his acquittal, was suddenly persona non grata, and his reputation was ruined. It was as though the town said to him, "Okay, we'll let you get away with this one murder. But you have to go now." Where did he go, and what happened to him? What happened to all the other friends, neighbors, reporters, law enforcement personnel and the attorneys?

One of the advantages of writing about a crime that occurred a decade shy of half a century ago is that one gets to see the end of the story. The following are the outcomes.

ROSEMARY McCORMICK died in 2009 at Flagler Hospital, and she is buried at the St. Augustine National Cemetery right down the street from where she lived on Marine Street. She lies next to her husband, Connie McCormick, who died in 1987. The funeral services were held at Trinity Episcopal.

LOCKE McCORMICK finished his last two years of college at Flagler, graduating in 1978. Since then, he has lived and worked in Jacksonville, mostly in the field of automobile sales and service. Presently, he works as an inventory analyst for a foreign car distributor.

PATRICIA STANFORD's friend HUNTER BARNETT got her MBA from Florida State University. In the 1990s, she was a budget analyst for the Florida governor's office of budgeting and planning, and today, she is a senior management analyst for the Florida Commission on Human Relations.

JEAN TROEMEL, the artist and Frances's and Athalia's neighbor, is still alive and in her nineties. She lives on Marine Street and has the same phone number she had in the 1970s. She was honored in May 2015 by the River House Art Society in St. Johns County with a tribute showing her artwork over the past two decades.

PATRICK LYNN, former editor of the *St. Augustine Record*, died in Valdez, Alaska, in 2011, where he distinguished himself by writing about the *Exxon Valdez* oil spill in 1989. He contacted former staffers Anne Heymen and Fred Whitley from the *Record* six months before he died, saying, "Some of my fondest memories were of St. Augustine." He requested "his ashes be spread

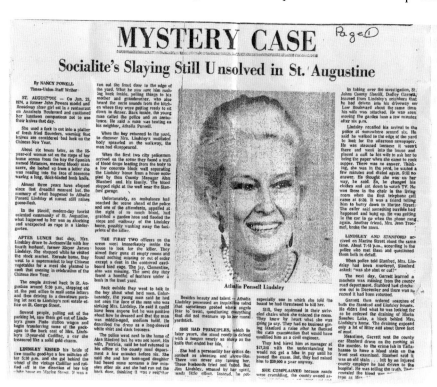

Nancy Powell's follow-up on her friend's case in 1976. *Courtesy of the Times-Union.*

in the Tolomato Cemetery in St. Augustine," as his wish was to rest among the "descendants of the Minorcans and conquistadors."

Nancy Powell, the *Florida Times-Union* newspaper reporter and friend to Athalia and Frances, retired to Gibsonton in southwest Florida. In 2005, she wrote a second book, *Murder on the Rocks*, set in Miami and the Florida Keys. If she is still alive, she is ninety years old. Jim Mast, her coauthor and publisher of *Bloody Sunset in St. Augustine*, died in Hastings, Florida, in 2015.

Record photographer Philip Whitley freelances as an on-call aerial photographer for fire rescue in St. Augustine.

Record reporter Anne Heymen is retired and enjoys traveling with friends and keeping up a local website, Totally St. Augustine.

Jackie Feagin, *Record* newspaper reporter and loyal friend of the Stanfords, refuses, in her own words, "to look back on the unhappy events surrounding the death of Mrs. Lindsley." Concerning the infamous crime she covered for the *Record*, she has declined requests to write a book and declined interviews with those who planned to write books and even television appearances, as she feels that "everything I know about the case is contained in my news articles."

In 1978, Frank Upchurch Jr. was appointed to the Fifth District Court of Appeals in Daytona Beach, where he served as a judge until he retired in 1988. He was one of the original trustees on the board of Flagler College, where he left an endowment to the law department. His grandson, Tracy, who served in the Florida House of Representatives, teaches law there. Frank died in 2012 as the result of a fall.

Judge Eugene Eastmoore served as a circuit judge until 1990, when he retired. He continued to live in Palatka and died in July 2015.

Assistant State Attorney Richard Watson was elected to the St. Augustine City Commission the same year that Alan Stanford was acquitted. He was appointed circuit judge for the Seventh Judicial Circuit from 1977 to 1996. In 2008, the St. Johns County Courthouse was renamed in his honor as the Richard O. Watson Judicial Center. Watson died in 2011.

State Attorney Stephen Boyles became a circuit judge in 1988. He wrote an autobiography of his life titled *The Country Jurist* in 2003. Jim Mast edited it. Boyles died in Putnam County in 2008, survived by his widow, Sally.

Walter Arnold endured a personal tragedy three months after Alan Stanford was acquitted. His beloved daughter, Terri, died at the age of thirty-one in May 1975. Walter worked until he was ninety and then dissolved the law firm of Booth and Arnold. He wrote his memoir, *Not Guilty*, in 2002. When asked if he believed in Alan's innocence, he quoted Clarence Darrow:

The Richard O. Watson Judicial Center. *Photo by Bob Randall.*

"I never asked him." Walter died at his home in Ponte Vedra Beach in 2009. He and his daughter are buried at Oak Lawn Cemetery in Jacksonville.

MICHAEL BOSS resigned his position as pastor of Trinity Episcopal in February 1975. He ended up in his hometown of Jacksonville as the pastor of St. Paul's

Episcopal, a church not far from the one Athalia attended and where her and her mother's funeral services were held. He died of cancer in 2012.

Former city of St. Augustine detective and sergeant DOMINIC NICKLO is enjoying his retirement with his wife, Betty. They divide their time between their home in St. Augustine, where they've lived for more than fifty-five years, and a property in the Carolinas.

Lieutenant EDDIE LIGHTSEY has left a legacy. A road bearing the Lightsey name cuts through the southwestern portion of town. A family business of Christmas tree stands still operates after thirty-five years. Yet bad press dogs the Lightsey name. Eddie's grandson, Ben, is in jail, convicted of beating and strangling his wife and then dumping her body in the Atlantic Ocean in an attempted cover-up. Eddie is still alive and living in St. Augustine.

FRANCIS O'LOUGHLIN served the City of St. Augustine Police Department for twenty-one years before beating Dudley Garrett in an election for St. Johns County sheriff in 1980. He served for four years and then moved to Green Cove Springs and joined the Clay County police force. He retired in 2001 and died in May 2015.

Sheriff DUDLEY GARRETT was defeated for reelection in 1980 after serving as sheriff for ten years. In 2007, Fred Green, former county commissioner, wrote a tribute to him in the *St. Augustine Record* saying in part:

> *I personally knew Garrett to be a dedicated crime fighter who never allowed politics or politicians to interfere with what he knew had to be done.*
>
> *His arrest of County Manager Alan Stanford in the 1974 murder of Athalia Ponsell Lindsley was an example of his lack of fear of stepping on the toes of political heavies. Though a jury acquitted Stanford after deliberating less than two hours over a mountain of evidence, Garrett remained certain he arrested the right man and closed the case.*
>
> *For the next 30 years of his life, he continued to firmly maintain the jury freed a guilty man.*

Sheriff Garrett died in Crestview, Florida, in 2007.

HENRY DUWARD "DEWEY" LEE is buried at Evergreen Cemetery in St. Augustine. A former colleague described him "as the best damn Ford mechanic I ever met." A U.S. veteran's medal and an American flag are affixed to his grave, which is engraved with a cross and the legend "Florida US Coast Guard World War II." Dewey died on Labor Day 1997.

HERBIE WILES served twelve years on the St. Johns County Commission. He is still alive, and so is his successful insurance business. His son, Doug Wiles, manages Herbie Wiles Insurance now, and Doug dabbles in local politics; he served as Florida House Representative for two years after Tracy Upchurch.

In 2013, St. Augustine mayor JOE BOLES awarded Herbie the Nineteenth Order of La Florida, a prestigious honor created in 1975 to recognize those who contributed extraordinary services to the community.

In 2013, Herbie dipped into local controversy once again when he was quoted in the *St. Augustine Record* concerning a local suicide that the *New York Times* and PBS *Frontline* were investigating as a murder. The St. Johns County Sheriff's Office ruled that the 2010 death of Michelle O'Connell, the twenty-four-year-old girlfriend of a deputy, was a suicide despite the fact that she died of a gunshot wound to the mouth even with another bullet lodged in the carpet next to her. The newspaper reporter likened the verdict to a cover-up similar to the "unsolved murder" of Athalia Ponsell Lindsley. Obviously, the reporter did not know the real history of Athalia's murder, for which the sheriff's office pursued justice and the media venerated the accused murderer.

Nevertheless, Herbie, who knew the deputy or knew of him, did not rush to judgment. He was quoted as saying, "I don't know what's fact or fiction."

FRANCES BEMIS clearly spent a lot of time pondering how to divide her assets, as her will was eight pages long. She appointed her lifelong friend, a Smith College graduate, Mary Louise Boyer, as her executor. Frances was quite specific in the dispersion of her assets.

In her will, Frances directed that there be no funeral or memorial service, and she donated her body to the College of Medicine at the University of Florida. She directed Mary to pay off all of her debts. There were pages of bequests, including phone numbers. Little Clay Martin received her collection of John F. Kennedy half dollars. Her friend Nancy Powell had her pick of Frances's paintings and a first-edition copy of *Gone with the Wind* autographed by Margaret Mitchell. Her neighbor artist Jean Troemel received all her art books. She even remembered her plumber, Clarence Thigpen, with a blue ashtray.

There were larger bequeaths. She left $100 to the historic Echo House, which served the Lincolnville Branch of the St. John's County Welfare Federation and whose restoration was a goal of her friend Rosalie Gordon-Mills. She left money to the St. Augustine Public Library on the condition that it use the $150 to "purchase books by black authors, including Maya Angelou's *I Know Why the Caged Bird Sings*."

Frances left money to the St. Augustine Art Center, provided the $100 was used for the membership of people who would like to join but couldn't afford the fee.

Maria Sanchez Apartments, where Frances Bemis lived. *Photo by Bob Randall.*

True to her word, Frances left a legacy to Bethune-Cookman College in her will. She bequeathed the profits from the sale of her house on Marine Street, as well as gave indication for the rest:

> *All the rest, residue, and remainder of the property which I may own at the time of my death, real, personal, and mixed, tangible and intangible, of whatsoever nature and whatsoever situated, including all lapsed legacies and devices, I bequeath to the scholarship fund of Bethune Cookman College, Daytona Beach, Florida to provide scholarships for worthy students from St. Augustine Florida. I request that scholarship applicants be screened and approved by Mrs. Rosalie Gordon-Mills of St. Augustine or if predeceased by Mr. Otis Mason.*

Frances's generous scholarship is still available to citizens of St. Augustine attending Bethune-Cookman University, an endowment covering one to four years of college and presided over by Mr. Otis Mason.

PATTI MULLEN STANFORD was the shred of hope that Alan's friends clung to during the damning, and convincing, evidence presented against him by the state prosecutors. There was no way that Stephen Boyles's accusation could be true—that Patti discovered her husband drenched in blood, machete in hand, in her own backyard. Her friends argued that Patti would never have stayed with Alan.

The Stanfords sold their home and left St. Augustine in 1975. First, they moved to Miami, where Alan found work. There were rumors that Patti and Alan separated at that point. But that really proves nothing—after the incredible strain of the murder trial, any marriage would suffer. Patti lived with Alan, or near him, in Mount Pleasant, South Carolina, where they eventually settled. They purchased a house and a condominium.

Patti was married to Alan when she died in 1987 of lung cancer, a week before her daughter Patricia's thirty-second birthday. Patti's final resting place in Mount Pleasant Memorial Gardens bears a plaque with her name, the dates of her birth and her death and the single engraved word *Beloved*. She lies to the right of Alan's grave. They are side by side for eternity.

To all appearances, it is the perfect ending of a long and loyal marriage and validates her friends' hopes of Alan's innocence. But there is a slight twist to the story. In 1980, Patti made out her own will, separate from Alan's. In it, she left everything to her daughters, Sherry, Patricia and Annette. If any of the girls died before Patti, she directed that her estate be divided among the surviving daughters. It was a significant amount of money. The fact that Alan was not included in the proceeds indicates that the money was hers alone. The fact that she left all her money to her daughters could be a clue as to why she stayed, and stayed silent, all those years.

Apparently, PERRY MULLEN provided for Patti and gave her some financial advice. Yet Patti still trusted Alan enough to make him the executor of her estate. That turned out to be a mistake.

PATRICIA STANFORD attended Clemson University, her father's alma mater, in 1975. At some point, she married and had children. She remained in South Carolina, close to her parents and to her sisters.

Then some disturbing events occurred. When Patti died and left all her money to her daughters, Alan waited only seventeen days before firing Ivan N. Nossokoff, Patti's lawyer and trustee. In a letter to the probate court, dated December 11, 1987, Mr. Nossokoff asked the court to remove his name as the attorney of record immediately. From then on, Alan administered Patti's estate on his own as the executor and trustee.

At first, Patricia did nothing about this. Her sister Annette was only fifteen years old and in Alan's custody. Her sister's expenses and her imminent college tuition needed to be paid for. The money was in stocks, and Patricia probably assumed that it would only appreciate. But within a year, Alan went through a significant amount of the money, with only a fraction of receipts recorded in official records.

According to court records, Patricia began asking for receipts. Alan didn't respond. Eventually, everyone hired lawyers. In October 1991, Patricia and Sherry filed against Alan in probate court trying to terminate his trustee status and issuing a restraining order. Alan fought back in November of the same year. Alan claimed that a handwritten note by Patti dated August 1, 1985, guaranteed him the trustee status.

By January 1992, Patricia had filed suit against Alan to have him dismissed as the executor of Patti's will. Her suit was settled out of court by July of that year and dismissed without prejudice. In signing the agreement, Alan had to turn in all his checkbooks, canceled checks and statements related to the trust fund to Patricia's lawyer. Then he had to "accompany" the lawyers to the bank to terminate his authority to sign checks on the account. The stock certificates were taken out of Alan's control.

Patricia was fair with Alan. She gave him the money for the sale of the house he owned with Patti. She reimbursed him for Annette's expenses. She paid for all the lawyers, including his. She paid him for "claims, fees, costs, and expenses incurred when he was the trustee." Then she made sure that money was put aside for Annette's college and ensured that the condominium was in Annette's name. When Annette turned twenty-five, all of the remaining funds would be divided equally between the three sisters.

Patricia assumed the emotionally wrenching role—first in her late teens and then in her early thirties—of navigating legal battles in which her father, Alan Griffith Stanford Jr., was at the center of controversy. The first legal trial Patricia endured with Alan led to his "victory." The second legal trial she endured with Alan led to Patti's vindication.

Although he still had a sister in Georgia, after leaving St. Augustine, ALAN STANFORD drifted to South Carolina—the southern state where he attended Clemson (and where he is still listed as an honorary alumnus) and a state, ironically, that topped the list of the Violence Policy Center as the number-one spot for murdering women. The *Charleston Post and Courier* won a Pulitzer in 2013 for its reporting on the subject.

Alan got a job as a marine engineer with the Charleston Naval Shipyard. It closed in 1994. By then, Alan was ready for retirement, and he was married to someone whom Walter Arnold, who kept in touch, referred to as "a charming lady." She was thirteen years younger than Alan and worked for an interior decorator, and the couple lived in a big house in Mount Pleasant, South Carolina. Alan was an usher and a lector at the Episcopal church. He

Alan's former home in Mount Pleasant, South Carolina. *Photo by Bob Randall.*

Alan and Patti Stanford's graves. *Photo by Bob Randall.*

Stanford bench at Mount Pleasant Memorial Gardens. *Photo by Bob Randall.*

worked part time as a substitute teacher in a local high school, tried ballroom dancing and traveled.

Alan had one more brief brush with the law in 2001 when he was arrested and fined for a criminal traffic deposition in Mount Pleasant. He died in his home of cancer on Labor Day 2006. He had quite a long obituary in the *Charleston Post and Courier.* "An avid sailor and boat builder, Stanford was one of the last great southern gentlemen…he was retired from the Charleston Naval Shipyard and held the designation of Professional Engineer…a wonderful husband and father, he was always involved in his daughter's lives." The obituary did not mention that Alan ever lived in Florida.

He is buried next to Patti at Mount Pleasant Memorial Gardens. A granite "STANFORD" bench faces the graves for relatives and friends to sit and mourn. His plaque notes that he served in the U.S. Merchant Marines in World War II and LTJC in the U.S. Navy. There is an engraved cross on the plaque and the following words all in caps: "LOVING HUSBAND, FATHER, FRIEND."

There is no shade near Alan's grave; it bakes in the sun. In a nearby juniper bush, a colony of yellow jackets swarms. In their predatory way, they swarm all around his grave.

JAMES "JINX" LINDSLEY lies at the foot of his first wife's grave. A simple plaque bearing his name and the dates of his birth and his death mark his final resting place. His parents and other relatives are buried in the plot with him.

A Catholic-Greek symbol carved into the headstone of a stone cross presides over the Lindsley family plot at Evergreen Cemetery in St. Augustine. The symbol looks like a capital P with an X intersecting its stem. Apparently, it is a symbol for the Byzantine emperor Constantine, who converted to Christianity. It means "conquer in the name of Christ."

In life, James was never a rich man. When he and Lillian were newly married, they boarded in the home of P.F. Carcaba, the man who established the first cigar factory in St. Augustine. Lillian worked as a dance

Top: Lindsley family plot at Evergreen Cemetery in St. Augustine. *Photo by Bob Randall.*

Left: Lillian and James Lindsley's graves. *Photo by Bob Randall.*

James Lindsley's unoccupied home in 2015. *Photo by Bob Randall.*

instructor throughout their marriage and choreographed her student's performances in city celebrations, such as *The Sword and the Stone.* Then she died, and two years later, James lost the election for the first time in a dozen years for his county commission seat. He married Athalia.

When Athalia died, he split the proceeds from the sale of her house on Marine Street with her sister, Geraldine. Then he sold the historic Lindsley family home on 214 St. George Street, where he ran his real estate business and where he used to work every day with Athalia.

A two-time widower, he retired to his home on Lew Street on Anastasia Island. He took in roomers and worked part time. He died in 1983. Perhaps he would be gratified to know that his house still stands, unoccupied but owned by his son, James R. Lindsley, on land that is worth $500,000 in today's market.

GERALDINE HORTON, sister of Athalia, died in Honolulu, Hawaii, in 1984.

If Athalia Ponsell Lindsley succeeded in her quest to run Alan Griffith Stanford Jr. out of town, he also succeeded in sending her back where she came from. The same pallbearers who served at her mother's funeral in April 1973 carried Athalia to her final rest less than a year later. She is buried at Oak Lawn Cemetery in Jacksonville, the cemetery where Walter Arnold and his daughter, Therese, are buried.

Number 214 St. George Street in 2015. *Photo by Bob Randall.*

Margherita Fetter's grave at Oak Lawn Cemetery in Jacksonville. *Photo by Bob Randall.*

Charles Fetter's grave at Oak Lawn Cemetery in Jacksonville. *Photo by Bob Randall.*

The commercial zone has crept up to the cemetery. The road to Oak Lawn is lined with restaurants, shops and strip malls. Some old neighborhoods survive—neighborhoods with iron railings leading up three steps to sturdy doors. At Oak Lawn, Athalia does not lie next to her mother and father, Margherita and Charles Fetter. They are in the row above her, and Athalia lies surrounded by strangers behind a fountain. Her plaque bears only her name and the date of her death.

One of the disturbing eventualities in writing about the crime that ended her life is that Athalia becomes a minor character in the narrative. In life, she loomed large. The best eulogy offered Athalia was on an Internet board in 2012 from a woman named Clara Waldhari, who was entering court transcripts from Athalia's murder trial on the website of a friend. She got to know Athalia from these records and offered a beautifully written summation of the life of a woman who was born too soon and died tragically:

> *Her friends and enemies called her intelligent. Of that, there was no question. Even the witnesses for the defense admitted that she routinely got the better, intellectually, and in every other way of Stanford. Did she have grace? Why*

Athalia's grave plaque. *Photo by Bob Randall.*

yes, I believe she did. She was a woman who had and held deep friendships, who had deeply held convictions—she was a proud and vocal conservative—who loved animals, who was no one's fool—and more. Might not qualify to you or to those with whom you've spoken. Does to me, however.

APL was savagely murdered, nearly decapitated, with a machete. I think that was the Message. Kill her, cut off her head—that was the only way to shut her up. Thing is, no one has really stopped talking about APL or her murder yet. Never will. Can't do a cold case on her, either. All the evidence was "mysteriously" destroyed.

It makes me sad to learn that APL is thought of so harshly. She was an "uppity woman" for those times, no doubt. I for one do NOT believe "she got what was coming to her."

It is no lie that the evidence for case no. 74-43CF, *The State of Florida v. Alan Griffith Stanford Jr.*, is gone. It did not, however, "mysteriously" disappear. Several cases were cleared out of the evidence room in 1988, and Alan's case was one of them. In the list of items thrown out, a "broken" wristwatch is noted.

Dudley Garrett was not sheriff in 1988 and neither was Francis O'Loughlin. However, Sheriff Garrett designated the case as "closed," not

The murder weapon and Alan Stanford's watch. *Courtesy of the St. Johns County Sheriff's Department. Photo by Bob Randall.*

"cold." The new sheriff was probably just trying to make room. According to the sheriff's office, the average retention for evidence is about ten years.

In 2011, the St. Johns County Sheriff's Office was awarded a grant from the U.S. Department of Justice for "Solving Cold Cases with DNA." Stephanie Eliot, a St. Johns County crime scene technician, said that eleven cold cases were investigated. Athalia Ponsell Lindsley's was not among them. For one thing, the sheriff's office never considered the case unsolved in spite of the verdict. For another, the evidence was gone. But even if the evidence was still there, it may not have been a good bet. The bloodstains on Alan's clothes were too compromised. The sheriff's office has a scoring system where it determines whether the DNA present is sufficient or if it too degraded by time or other testing methods. So it used the grant money on more recent cases.

The hair samples are another story. If they could have been verified as Athalia's hair—by twenty-first-century standards—who knows what that could have led to. In Frances Bemis's cold case, "brown Caucasian hairs" that were not hers were found at the scene of the crime. These were not DNA tested either.

Real life produces an outcome so unlike fiction. Often there is no resolution. Events build up to a climax and then just dwindle away. There are no confessions, no tying up of loose ends. The horror that struck still echoes—a faint remembrance, the edge of nightmare, cloven footsteps in the distance.

So much of life is secret. There are the big secrets—what happens before birth and after death. There are the small secrets—day-to-day ruminations, barely suppressed impulses, the urges that run beneath the bloodline motivating our every move. Perhaps some secrets are never meant to be known.

Or perhaps they are. What happens to a secret, a big one, when it emerges from the darkness and into the light? Does it dry up, desiccate and fly off in a million bits into the universe? Does it lose its dominating power? Is the reality of a fact less compelling than the power of a secret?

Yes, there is power in keeping a secret, but it pales before the power of a truth. Truth leads to understanding and to justice. There are still people living who could provide evidence in really "closing" the case of Athalia's murder. Perhaps the events set into motion during that long-ago January afternoon linger because of a karmic imbalance resulting from the lack of resolution.

Since the controversy concerning this case has not gone away, there is still time—there is always time—for the truth. There is still time to answer the question, "Would the truth put this case to rest?"

Perhaps Athalia is still waiting for the "mystery" to be solved.

BIBLIOGRAPHY

BOOKS, CENSUS RECORDS, POLICE REPORTS, PERIODICALS, JOURNALS AND MISCELLANEOUS DATA

Affidavit for Search Warrant. 126 Marine Street. "Affiant, Sheriff Dudley Garrett, Jr." Granted by County Judge Charles Mathis, January 25, 1974. [St. Augustine.]

Arnold, Walter G. *Not Guilty: The Autobiography of Walter G. Arnold.* N.p., 2001.

Belleville, Bill. *Deep Cuba: The Inside Story of an American Oceanographic Expedition.* Athens: University of Georgia Press, 2002.

Bemis, Frances. Last Will and Testament. St. Augustine, October 16, 1974. St. Johns County Sheriff's Office evidence.

Boyles, Stephen L. *The Life and Times of a Country Jurist.* Orlando, FL: McFadden, 2003.

Buss, David M. *The Murder Next Door: Why the Mind Is Designed to Kill.* New York: Penguin Press, 2005.

Campbell, Jacquelyn C., PhD, RN. "Risk Factors for Femicide in Abusive Relationships: Results from a Multisite Case Control Study." *American Journal of Public Health* (2003).

Circuit Court of the Seventh Judicial Circuit, in and for St. Johns County, Florida. Captain R.M. Williams deposition. Case no. 74-43CF. St. Johns County Courthouse, St. Augustine, Florida, June 20, 1974.

———. Daniel B. Wilson deposition. Case no. 74-43CF. St. Johns County Courthouse, St. Augustine, Florida, February 12, 1974.

————. David Allen Wehking deposition. Case no. 74-43CF. St. Johns County Courthouse, St. Augustine, Florida, February 1, 1974.

————. Dominic Frank Nicklo deposition. Case no. 74-43CF. St. Johns County Courthouse, St. Augustine, Florida, June 21, 1974.

————. Dudley W. Garrett Jr. deposition. Case no. 74-43CF. St. Johns County Courthouse, St. Augustine, Florida, June 20, 1974.

————. Eddie Roy Lightsey deposition. Case no. 74-43CF. St. Johns County Courthouse, St. Augustine, Florida, June 21, 1974.

————. Floyd Russell Hardin deposition. Case no. 74-43CF. St. Johns County Courthouse, St. Augustine, Florida, February 12, 1974.

————. Freddie Leroy Hudnall deposition. Case no. 74-43CF. St. Johns County Courthouse, St. Augustine, Florida, February 1, 1974.

————. Geraldine Horton deposition. Case no. 74-43CF. St. Johns County Courthouse, St. Augustine, Florida, June 21, 1974.

————. Hazel McCallum deposition. Case no. 74-43CF. St. Johns County Courthouse, St. Augustine, Florida, February 26, 1974.

————. Henry Duward Lee deposition. Case no. 74-43CF. St. Johns County Courthouse, St. Augustine, Florida, June 20, 1974.

————. James S. Lindsley deposition. Case no. 74-43CF. St. Johns County Courthouse, St. Augustine, Florida, June 21, 1974.

————. Jesse Osgrove Miller deposition. Case no. 74-43CF. St. Johns County Courthouse, St. Augustine, Florida, February 27, 1974.

————. Kenneth Henry Beeson Jr. deposition. Case no. 74-43CF. St. Johns County Courthouse, St. Augustine, Florida, February 27, 1974.

————. Miss Hunter Barnett deposition. Case no. 74-43CF. St. Johns County Courthouse, St. Augustine, Florida, February 27, 1974.

————. Miss Jody Hough deposition. Case no. 74-43CF. St. Johns County Courthouse, St. Augustine, Florida, February 26, 1974.

————. Miss Patricia Stanford deposition. Case no. 74-43CF. St. Johns County Courthouse, St. Augustine, Florida, February 1, 1974.

————. "Motion for Change of Venue." Case no. 74-43 CF. *State of Florida v. Alan Stanford, Defendant.* Filed by Richard O. Watson, Assistant State Attorney, April 16, 1974.

————. "Motion to Suppress." Case no. 74-43 CF. *State of Florida v. Alan Stanford, Jr.* Filed by Walter Arnold Jr., attorney for defendant, March 29, 1974.

————. Mrs. Allen Stanford deposition. Case no. 74-43CF. St. Johns County Courthouse, St. Augustine, Florida, February 26, 1974.

———. Notarized Statement for Francis M. O'Loughlin. Re: Change of Venue. In the Circuit Court, in and for St. Johns County, Florida, Case no. 74-43 CF. *State of Florida v. Alan G. Stanford, Jr. Defendant.* April 11, 1974.

———. Notarized Statement for Nancy S. Powell. Re: Change of Venue. In the Circuit Court, in and for St. Johns County, Florida, Case no. 74-43 CF. *State of Florida v. Alan G. Stanford, Jr. Defendant.* April 16, 1974.

———. Ray Virgil Fox deposition. Case no. 74-43CF. St. Johns County Courthouse, St. Augustine, Florida, February 12, 1974.

———. "Traverse and Answer to State's Motion for Change of Venue." Case no. 74-43 CF. *State of Florida v. Alan Stanford, Jr., Defendant.* Filed by attorneys for defendant, by Walter Arnold Jr., April 25, 1974.

———. William Carl Tipton Jr. deposition. Case no. 74-43CF. St. Johns County Courthouse, St. Augustine, Florida, February 12, 1974.

Colburn, David R. *Racial Change and Community Crisis: St. Augustine, Florida, 1877–1980.* New York: Columbia University Press, 1985.

Commissioners Minutes. Book 1, Disk 1, no. 1, page 110. Signed by H. Wiles, Chairman [St. Johns County], February 25, 1974. CD.

———. Book 1, Disk 11, no. 5, page 633. [St. Johns County] October 9, 1973. CD.

———. Book 1, Disk 11, no. 5, page 76. [St. Johns County] January 22, 1974. CD.

———. Book 1, Disk 12, no. 3, page 104. [St. Johns County] February 12, 1974. CD.

———. Z, Disk 13, no. 10, pages 698, 700–702. [St. Johns County] November 13, 1973. CD.

"Conversation Between Mr. Alan Stanford, Off. P.E. McIntire & Lt. C.G. Cannon." Reported to Officer Terrell Davis. [St. Augustine.] January 25, 1974.

Daly, Martin, and Wilson, Margo. *Homicide.* New Brunswick, NJ: Transaction Publishers, 1988.

Davis, Terrell. Complaint Report. *Murder Investigation of Mrs. Lindsley.* "Mrs. Genie C. Dodd. Rep. no. 10109." 330 Charlotte Street, St. Augustine, Florida, January 24, 1974.

———. Complaint Report. *Murder Investigation of Mrs. Lindsley.* "Rep. no. 10109." St. Augustine, Florida, January 27, 1974. Sheriff Garret and officer met with Detective Jenkins at Daytona Beach Police Department.

Desco Marine. "Fox Welding signature." Truck Log, January 23, 1974.

"Dr. Peter Lipkovic Examination Report." ME 74-1438, Bemis, Frances, November 1974. St. Johns County Sheriff's Office evidence archive.

Evidence for Disposal. Rep. no. 74-43CF. St. Augustine, St. Johns County Sheriff's Office, 1988. Lists evidence from the Lindsley case marked for disposal in March 1988.

Federal Bureau of Investigation, Florida Department of Criminal Law Enforcement. FBI File No. 95-196554. Re: Gerald Austin and Alan Stanford, suspects; Frances Bemis, victim; Investigation of Death. Attn: Mr. Dennis Fischer, special agent. Jacksonville, Florida, January 10, 1975.

Florida State Census, 1867–1945, 1935. C.F. Fetter [Duval County], Precinct 15 (database online).

Forum, Florida Humanities Council 35, no. 3. "Dreams Lost, Dreams Found in the Quest for Florida" (Fall 2011): 6.

Fox, M. James Alan, and Marianne W. Zawitz. "Homicide Trends in the United States." Bureau of Justice, July 1, 2007.

Frances Bemis Papers, 1921–1974. Sophia Smith Collection. Smith College, Northampton, Massachusetts. In particular "Photographs, Frances Bemis," 1947, Box 1, Folder 3; "General Correspondence," 1947, Box 3, Folder 2; "Older Woman Alone" (notes and research materials, 1967–70; and notes and research material, clippings and notes re: celebrities, models and "personalities" with whom Bemis worked, notes from agent and typescript and personal notes, 1943–70), Box 4, Folders 15, 16 and 19, and Box 4, Folder 15, 1933–54, Folder 16, 1943, 1959, and Folder 19, 1970s, and Folder 21; "Civil Rights," 1960s, Box 13, Folder 18; "The Florida Story," "Organization for Improved St. George St.," miscellaneous clippings (includes articles by Bemis), St. Augustine Historical Society miscellany, pamphlets and brochures, 1956–71, Box 12, Folders 14, 16, 24, 25, 26 and 27; "Civil Rights," Box 13, Folder 18.

Inventory and Return. Dudley W. Garrett Jr. Results of Search Warrant. 126 Marine Street, St. Augustine, Florida, January 25, 1974.

Investigative Report. Homicide, Serial No. E17560. "Of Mrs. Martha Davis by Plt. Jimmy S. Hewitt." [St. Augustine.] November 4, 1974

———. Murder, Serial No. E7330. Officers assigned Deputy Cannon, O'Loughlin, Investigator Nicklo, Lieutenant Duhon, Robinson, Dobbs, Janson, Larrow, Bissell. 124 Marine Street, St. Augustine, Florida. January 23, 1974.

Letter from Athalia Ponsell Lindsley to Mr. J.Y. Read, Executive Director, St. Augustine, December 4, 1973.

Letter from Elmer Emrich to "Mrs. Athalia Ponsell Lindsley, St. Augustine, December 17, 1973.

Letter from Frances Bemis to Sheriff Dudley Garrett, St. Augustine, February 13, 1974. Speculating that an unsolved murder in Irvington, New York, resembled Athalia's.

Letter from George B. Stallings Jr. to Mr. Elmer Emrich, Jacksonville, January 15, 1974.

Letter from Ira L. Inman, Deputy Clerk, to Sheriff Dudley Garrett, St. Augustine, February 4, 1974.

Letter from J.Y. Read to George B. Stallings, St. Augustine, January 17, 1974.

Midships Yearbook, 1945. "Alan G. Stanford, Jr." United States Merchant Marine Academy, Kings Point, New York.

Mier, Russell T., and Hazel M. McCormack Complaint Report. *Murder Investigation of Mrs. Lindsley.* "Rep. no. 10119. St. Augustine: Captain Auxiliary Services, 1974." Mr. Mier drove down Marine Street right after the murder and didn't see anyone on the street.

Mitchell, Florence S. *Sacred to the Memory: A History of the Huguenot Cemetery, 1821–1884, St. Augustine, Florida.* St. Augustine, FL: Friends of the Huguenot Cemetery, 1998.

1940 Census record. Census Place: New York, New York, New York. Roll T627_2648, page 2B. Enumeration District, 31-1016, Athalia and Geraldine Ponsell.

1930 Census record. Census Place: Atlanta, Fulton, Georgia. Roll 365, page 5A. Enumeration District 0185. Image 329.0. FHL microfilm: 2340100, Alan G. Stanford, Jr.

Nolan, David. *The Houses of St. Augustine.* Sarasota, FL: Pineapple, 1995.

Offense Report, Officer Lennon. "Arrest of Thad Jude Rutowski." 1227 So. Atlantic, Daytona Beach, Florida, 6:52 p.m., January 26, 1974.

Office of the Medical Examiner. Record of Identification of Body (Frances Bemis). "Mr. Charles Bennett." [St. Augustine.] November 6, 1974

———. Record of Identification of Body (Frances Bemis). "Mrs. Nancy Powell. [St. Augustine.] November 6, 1974.

Osborn, Albert Sherman. *Proof of Handwriting.* Kessinger Legacy Reprints. N.p.: Kessinger Publishing LLC, 1912.

Patricia Angela Stanford G-, plaintiff, et al. v. Alan Griffith Stanford Jr, defendant, et al. Charleston County Clerk of Court, State of South Carolina, In the Court of Common Pleas Ninth Judicial Circuit Case no. 92-CP-10-0283. December 8, 1992. Microfilm.

Powell, Nancy (Nancy Smith), and Jim Mast. *Bloody Sunset in St. Augustine: A True Story.* East Palatka, FL: Federal Point Pub., 1998.

Rapaport, Elizabeth. "Staying Alive: Executive Clemency, Equal Protection, and the Politics of Gender in Women's Capital Cases." *Buffalo Criminal Law Review* 4, no. 2 (2001).

Sanford Crime Laboratory Report, Case no. 75-13609. Trace Investigation: Gerald Austin/suspect, Frances Bemis/victim. Examined by Steven R. Platt, criminologist; William H. Ragsdale, laboratory director. Sanford, Florida, May 9, 1975. Analysis of piece of denim material for presence of blood or seminal material. Nothing of further evidentiary value was present.

Shatz, Steven F., and Naomi R. Shatz. "Chivalry Is Not Dead: Murder, Gender, and the Death Penalty." *Berkeley Journal of Gender, Law and Justice* 27, no. 1 (2012). University of San Francisco Law Research Paper, no. 2011-08 (February 19, 2011).

South Carolina v. Alan Griffith Stanford Jr. Case no. 93634BW. Criminal Traffic; arrested by Officer David E. West, November 11, 2001.

St. Augustine, Florida Board of County Commissioners, St. Johns County. *Minutes Books 01, Y, Z, Feb. 72–Dec. 74.* St. Johns County Minutes and Records. CD.

St. Johns County Jail Log. "Special Visitors, Alan Stanford." [St. Augustine.] February 23–25, 1974.

Stanford, Alan G., Jr. Obituary. *Charleston Post and Courier*, September 9, 2006.
———. Résumé. Maryland, Hagerstown, 1968.

Stanford, Patricia Mullen. Last Will and Testament. Mount Pleasant, South Carolina, June 20, 1980.

Statement by Mrs. Elizabeth Williams, taken by Lieutenant Eddie Lightsey. 323 Charlotte Street, St. Augustine, Florida, September 14, 1974, 12:30 p.m.

Supplementary Investigative Report. Locke McCormick. Investigating Officer Joe Larrow. St. Augustine, Florida, January 23, 1974.
———. Murder. "Mrs. Allen Stanford." Investigating Officer Joe Larrow. St. Augustine, Florida, January 23, 1974. Call no. E-7330.
———. Murder. "Virginia Wrigley." Investigating Officer Dominic Nicklo and Dennis Fischer, Florida Department of Law Enforcement. St. Augustine, Florida, November 4, 1974. Call no. E-17560.

Wells, William K., and Ann Wells. *Viva O'Brien*. Music by Marie Grever and lyrics by Raymond Leveen. Majestic Theatre on Broadway, New York, October 9–25, 1941. Twenty performances, with Athalia Ponsell as the Senorita 9, sang with ensemble "Our Song").

NEWSPAPER ARTICLES

(Charleston, SC) Post and Courier. "Stanford, Alan G. Jr. Obituary." September 8, 2006.

(Elyria, OH) Chronicle Telegram. "'Hate' Motive Seen in Brutal Slaying of Former Actress." January 25, 1974. Microfilm.

Drake, Frances. "Your Individual Horoscope: Aquarius." *St. Augustine Record,* January 24, 1974. Microfilm.

———. "Your Individual Horoscope: Aquarius, Leo." *St. Augustine Record,* January 23, 1974. Microfilm.

Feagin, Jackie. "Athalia: A Woman of Mystery, Controversy, Charm." *St. Augustine Record,* January 22, 1989.

Feagin, Jackie, and Mike Rolleston. "Murder Upsetting, but Most Do Not Fear for Safety." *St. Augustine Record,* January 1, 1974.

Florida Times-Union. "Charles Fetter Dies at Home in Riverside." May 30, 1937, 33. Microfilm.

———. "Lindsley, Athalia Obituary." January 27, 1974. Microfilm.

———. "A New Treaty with Cuba." June 2, 1934. Microfilm.

———. "Services Today for Mrs. Fetter." April 28, 1973. Microfilm.

Guinta, Peter. "A Recurring Horror." *St. Augustine Record,* January 29, 2007.

Hagood, Dick. "Lindsley: She Had No Enemies—Except One." *Florida Times-Union,* February 1, 1974. Microfilm.

Harris, David. "New Cold-Case Task Force Started by Florida Sheriff's Association." *Orlando Sentinel,* August 21, 2015.

Kilgallen, Dorothy. "Dorothy Kilgallen." *Lowell Sun,* June 5, 1945, 53. Microfilm. "Athalia Ponsell and Ken MacSarin, set to wed, decided uh-uh."

Leitao, Rachel. "St. Johns County Sheriff's Office Awarded 'Solving Cold Cases with DNA 'Grant.'" *First Coast News,* October 26, 2011.

Love, Susan. "Witness Places Lee at Scene—Mrs. Stanford Also Testifies in Thursday Proceedings." *St. Augustine Record,* January 31, 1975. Microfilm.

Lynn, Patrick. "Alan Stanford Arrest Ends Murder Suspense." *St. Augustine Record,* February 23–24, 1974.

———. "Lawmen Continue Hunt for Clues in Murder." *St. Augustine Record,* February 9–10, 1974. Microfilm.

———. "Pressure Has Been Enormous." *St. Augustine Record,* February 1, 1974.

———. "Stanford Granted $20,000 Bond After Entering Innocent Plea." *St. Augustine Record,* February 26, 1974. Microfilm.

———. "Stanford, Lindsley Both Pass Lie Detector Tests in Murder." *St. Augustine Record*, February 4, 1974.

Mansfield News-Journal. "Colonelcy? Well, the Sergeant Had a Nice Date, at Any Rate." January 30, 1942, 7. Microfilm. Athalia described as "face and figure" girl.

Mills, Roy. "Bloody Evidence Entered in Stanford Murder Trial." *Florida Times-Union,* January 29, 1975, A-1. Microfilm.

———. "Jury Acquits Stanford of Murder." *Florida Times-Union*, February 4, 1975, A-1. Microfilm.

———. "Lindsley Case Eyewitnessed?" *Florida Times-Union*, January 24, 1975, A-1. Microfilm.

———. "No Motive to Murder, Stanford Insists." *Florida Times-Union*, February 1, 1975, A-1. Microfilm.

———. "Stanford Grilled; Summations Are Due Monday." *Florida Times-Union*, February 2, 1975, A-1. Microfilm.

———. "Stanford Links to Killing Said Blood, Machete." *Florida Times-Union,* January 26, 1975, B-4. Microfilm.

———. "Stanford's Wife Gives Alibi; Witness Says Lee in Yard." *Florida Times-Union,* January 31, 1975, B-2. Microfilm.

———. "State Attorney Says Harassment by Mrs. Lindsley Led to Murder." *Florida Times-Union,* January 23, 1975, B-2. Microfilm.

———. "State Rests in Stanford Trial." *Florida Times-Union*, January 30, 1975. Microfilm.

———. "Witness Not Sure of Man's Identity." *Florida Times-Union,* January 25, 1975. Microfilm.

Mitchell, Paul. "Blood Near Scene Same as Victim's—Crime Lab Experts Take Stand." *St. Augustine Record,* January 29, 1975. Microfilm.

———. "Defense: Other Suspects, Leads Ignored—State 'Out to Get' Stanford." *St. Augustine Record,* January 30, 1975. Microfilm.

———. "Defense Questions Lindsley About Machete." *St. Augustine Record*, January 27, 1975. Microfilm.

———. "Jury Hears Grisly Murder Details." *St. Augustine Record,* January 23, 1975. Microfilm.

———. "Jury Selection Begins." *St. Augustine Record*, January 20, 1975. Microfilm.

———. "Jury Selection Continues." *St. Augustine Record*, January 21, 1975. Microfilm.

———. "Key Question: Where Was Stanford?" *St. Augustine Record,* January 25–26, 1975. Microfilm.

————. "Stanford Denies Feud with Mrs. Lindsley." *St. Augustine Record,* February 1–2, 1975. Microfilm.

————. "Stanford Jury Selected." *St. Augustine Record,* January 22, 1975. Microfilm.

————. "Stanford Takes Stand in His Own Defense." *St. Augustine Record,* January 31, 1975. Microfilm.

————. "State Introduces Machete in Murder Trial: Defense Tries to Implicate Finder." *St. Augustine Record,* January 28, 1975. Microfilm.

————. "State Says Articles Stanford's—Laundry Owner, Jeweler Testify." *St. Augustine Record,* January 29, 1975. Microfilm.

————. "State Witness Seems Vague." *St. Augustine Record,* January 24, 1975. Microfilm.

————. "Verdict May Come Tonight—Stanford Trial in the Midst of Summations." *St. Augustine Record,* February 3, 1975. Microfilm.

New Smyrna News. "Say Americans Are Persecuted on Isle." July 4, 1924. Microfilm. "Mrs. Charles F. Fetter protesting against ratification of the treaty under which Cuba would be given jurisdiction of the island."

Olean Evening Times. "Seditious Movement Is Practically Ended." May 10, 1924, 1. Microfilm. C.F. Fetter American citizens persecuted in the Isle of Pines; C.F. Fetter convicted, pardoned, released.

Ormond, Merri Vale. "Letters to the Editor: A Certain Spirit of Care." *St. Augustine Record,* January 23, 1974. Microfilm.

Osborne, Pete. "Something Was Wrong." *St. Augustine Record,* November 4, 1974. Microfilm.

Powell, Nancy. "Brutal Slaying Sends a Wave of Fear Across Ancient City." *Florida Times-Union,* February 1, 1974, B-2. Microfilm.

————. "Socialite's Slaying Still Unsolved in St. Augustine." *Florida Times-Union,* November 23, 1976, *Jacksonville Journal* section.

————. "Stanford Grand Jury Probe Continues in Old City Today." *Florida Times-Union,* March 1, 1974. Microfilm.

————. "Stanford Granted 'Indefinite' Leave." *Florida Times-Union,* February 26, 1974. Microfilm.

Russo, Harry. "Identity of Slayer Remains Controversial." *St. Augustine Record,* January 23, 1989.

————. "Murder Memories Still Scar." *St. Augustine Record,* January 22, 1989.

Sourgel, Matt. "St. Augustine Dwellers Are Careful with Conversation About Suicide Ruling." *St. Augustine Record,* December 8, 2013.

St. Augustine Record. "Condition of County Roads Is Criticized." October 10, 1973, 16.

———. "Editorial: Common Sense in Wake of Tragedy." February 15, 1974. Microfilm.

———. "Elks Name Students of the Month: Hunter Barnett, James McAdams Honored." January 23, 1974. Microfilm.

———. "F.D. Upchurch Is Honored by Kiwanis Int." January 23, 1974. Microfilm.

———. "$500 Offered to Person Finding Murder Weapon." February 16, 1974. Microfilm.

———. "Murder Probe Continues as Maria Sanchez Lake Drained." January 29, 1974. Microfilm.

———. "Police Find No New Clues." November 5, 1974. Microfilm.

———. "Police Offer $500 Reward." November 6, 1974. Microfilm. Sheriff Garrett offers reward for information about Frances Bemis's murder.

Stevens, Christine. "Judge Denies Acquittal Motion; State Rests Case." *St. Augustine Record*, January 30, 1975. Microfilm.

———. "Jury Hears Excerpts of Victim's Letters." *St. Augustine Record*, February 3, 1975. Microfilm.

———. "Stanford Is Acquitted." *St. Augustine Record*, February 4, 1975. Microfilm.

———. "Stanford Questioned About 'Feud' with Mrs. Lindsley." *St. Augustine Record*, February 1–2, 1975. Microfilm.

Strickland, Sandy. "'74 Slaying Still Stirs Emotions." *Florida Times-Union*, January 31, 2000.

Tebault, Hoopie. "Across the Desk." *St. Augustine Record*, March 2–3, 1974. Microfilm.

Times-Union Bureau. "Element of Time Puzzling in Trial." *Florida Times-Union*, February 1, 1975, *Jacksonville Journal* section.

———. "1st Witness to Mark Slaying Anniversary." *Florida Times-Union*, January 23, 1975, B-2. Microfilm.

———. "Lindsley Killer Hunt Continues in Old City." *Florida Times-Union*, January 27, 1974. Microfilm.

Washington Post. "Mrs. Charles Fetter and Mrs. Harriet Wheeler, of the Isle of Pines, Who Want the Little Island Kept Under the Flag of the United States." December 21, 1924. Microfilm. "A treaty, awaiting ratification for 21 years, acknowledges the sovereignty of Cuba over the island."

Winchell, Walter. "On Broadway." *North Adams Transcript*, June 29, 1942, 7. Microfilm. "The Lt. F. Baeler-Athalia Ponsell wedding set for yesterday is off for good."

Woolverton, Dave. "City Woman Slain." *St. Augustine Record*, November 4, 1974. Microfilm.

INTERVIEWS AND INTERVIEW REPORT FORMS

Best, Ronald. Interview conducted by Dominic Nicklo. January 26, 1974, 10:05 a.m.

Boyles, Sally, widow of former St. Johns County state attorney. Personal interview, June 19, 2015.

Brunson, B.O. Interview conducted by Sergeant Dominic Nicklo. 101 Marine Street, St. Augustine, Florida, 10:20 a.m., January 25, 1974.

Dodd, Mrs. Genie C. Interview conducted by Eddie Lightsey. 26 Willow Drive, St. Augustine, Florida, January 25, 1974. No. 10109.

Eliot, Stephanie, crime scene technician, St. Johns County. Telephone interview, June 23, 2015.

Fagen, Mrs. A.A. Interview conducted by Officer F.M. O'Loughlin. 321 St. George Street, St. Augustine, Florida, January 23, 1974. Call no. E-7330.

Gay, Mrs. Mary. Interview conducted by E.R Lightsey. Buckner Foundation, Jacksonville, Florida, March 7, 1974. CR No. 10109.

Hemmerson, Harold. Interview conducted by E.R. Lightsey. [St. Augustine.] March 7, 1974. CR No. 10109.

Heymen, Anne, retired reporter from the *St. Augustine Record*. Personal interview, June 15, 2015.

Keiereber, Victor. Interview conducted by E.R Lightsey. [St. Augustine.] March 1, 1974. CR No. 10109.

Mast, Jim, author of *Bloody Sunset in St. Augustine*. Personal interview, June 19, 2015.

Miller, Mr. Bud, polygraph examiner. Interview conducted by Captain R.M. Williams per telephone. St. Augustine, Florida, February 25, 1974.

Murphy, Mr. Thomas J., Jr. Interview Report Form, interview conducted by Special Agent Dallas Herring. [St. Augustine.] February 1, 1974. Case no. 523-1A-0016.

Nicklo, Dominic, retired St. Augustine Police Detective. Personal interview, June 18, 2015.

Odell, Quentin. Interview conducted by Eddie Lightsey. 26 Willow Drive, St. Augustine, Florida, January 25, 1974. No. 10109.

Parker, Mrs. Ruth. Interview Report Form, interview conducted by Special Agent Dallas Herring. [St. Augustine.] January 25, 1974. Case no. 523-1A-0016.

Powell, Gary. Interview conducted by Special Agent Dallas Herring. Daytona Beach, Florida, February 7, 1974. Case no. 523-1A-0016.

Shropshire, Mrs. Kathleen. Interview Report Form, interview conducted by Lieutenant Eddie Lightsey. [St. Augustine.] November 7, 1974.

Snow, John R. Interview conducted by Special Agent Dallas Herring. Levy-Wolf Department Store, West Adams Street, Jacksonville, Florida, February 1, 1974. Case no. 523-1A-0016.

Stanford, Dixon. Interview Report Form, interview conducted by Officer Terrell Davis. [St. Augustine.] January 25, 1974.

Stanford, Miss Patricia. Interview conducted by F.M. O'Loughlin. 126 Marine Street, St. Augustine, Florida, January 23, 1974, 7:35 p.m.

Stanford, Mrs. Allen. Interview conducted by Officer Dominic Nicklo. 126 Marine Street, St. Augustine, Florida, January 24, 1974, 9:45 a.m.

Townsend, Joe, Special Agent, FDLE, polygraph expert. Interview Report Form, interview conducted by Special Agent Dallas Herring. [St. Augustine.] February 5, 1974. Case no. 523-1A-0016.

Troemel, Jean, neighbor of Frances Bemis. Telephone interview, June 15, 2015.

Trull, Mrs. Mildred. Interview conducted by Special Agent Dallas Herring. Levy-Wolf Department Store, West Adams Street, Jacksonville, Florida, February 1, 1974. Case no. 523-1A-0016.

Wells, Charles L., Jr. Interview conducted by Special Agent Dallas Herring. Wells Jewelers, Jacksonville, Florida, February 1, 1974. Case no. 523-1A-0016.

Whitley, Philip, retired *St. Augustine Record* photographer. Personal Interview. June 8, 2015.

INDEX

Y

yellow fever 20

Z

Zales Jewelers 85
Zoric Cleaners 93
Zsa Zsa (Margherita's dog) 45, 47, 123

ABOUT THE AUTHOR

Elizabeth Randall is a widely published freelance writer and a high school English teacher. She is the author of four books. Her most recent publication was a book about history and folklore titled *Women in White: The Haunting of Northeast Florida*. She and her husband, Bob, who is a freelance photographer and who contributed many of the pictures in this book, divide their time between two homes: one in Lake Mary and one in Crystal River on the island of Ozello.